Writing Menopause

Published in Canada by
Inanna Publications and Education Inc.
210 Founders College, York University
4700 Keele Street, Toronto, Ontario M3J 1P3
Telephone: (416) 736-5356 Fax (416) 736-5765
Email: inanna.publications@inanna.ca Website: www.inanna.ca

| Canada Council for the Arts | Conseil des Arts du Canada | ONTARIO ARTS COUNCIL CONSEIL DES ARTS DE L'ONTARIO an Ontario government agency un organisme du gouvernement de l'Ontario | Canada |

The publisher gratefully acknowledges the support of the Canada Council for the Arts and the Ontario Arts Council for its publishing program. We also acknowlege the financial assistance of the Government of Canada through the Canada Book Fund.

Note from the publisher: Care has been taken to trace the ownership of copyright material used in this book. The author and the publisher welcome any information enabling them to rectify any references or credits in subsequent editions.

Cover artwork: Maria Wakefield
Cover design: Val Fullard

Library and Archives Canada Cataloguing in Publication

    Writing menopause : An anthology of fiction, poetry and creative nonfiction / edited by Jane Cawthorne and E. D. Morin.

(Inanna poetry and fiction series)
Issued in print and electronic formats.
ISBN 978-1-77133-353-5 (softcover). — ISBN 978-1-77133-354-2 (epub). — ISBN 978-1-77133-355-9 (kindle). — ISBN 978-1-77133-356-6 (pdf)

    1. Menopause — Literary collections. 2. Canadian literature (English) — 21st century. 3. American literature — 21st century. I. Cawthorne, Jane, 1962–, editor II. Morin, E. D. (Elaine D.), 1964–, editor III. Series: Inanna poetry and fiction series

PS8237.M46W75 2017   C810.8'03561   C2017-900324-0
                                                    C2017-900325-9

MIX
Paper from
responsible sources
FSC
www.fsc.org   FSC® C004071

Printed and Bound in Canada.

Writing Menopause

An Anthology of
Fiction, Poetry and Creative Nonfiction

edited by
Jane Cawthorne and E. D. Morin

INANNA Publications and Education Inc.
Toronto, Canada

Table of Contents

Acknowledgements

The shortness of time was poignantly brought to our attention twice during the making of this book with the losses of two of our contributors to cancer. Frances Hern died in September 2015, and Tanya Coovadia in May 2016. We wish that they could have held this book in their hands, seen their work in print, and enjoyed the moment that is so special to every writer.

Thank you:

To our writing community, particularly Lori Hahnel and Kari Strutt, for helping us get this book started, and for all those who encouraged us throughout the process.

To all of the writers who submitted to this anthology.

To our contributors whose individual works made this book possible and who have been unfailingly supportive.

To the Society for Menstrual Cycle Research for welcoming us at your 2015 conference.

To Maria Wakefield whose cover artwork has been the face of the anthology from the beginning.

To Crabapple Mews Collective, for being a place for us to collaborate.

To Lou Morin who offered us her keen editorial eye as well as a contribution to the collection.

To Inanna Publications and Luciana Ricciutelli, who said yes and who made the manuscript as good as it is through her impeccable editing lens.

To our partners who make our writing life possible.

Introduction

JANE CAWTHORNE AND E. D. MORIN

Menopause. Say the word in public. See what happens.

You may catch some knowing glances, a few rolled eyes, a few exasperated sighs. As Jane Silcott writes, you may see some *squinching*. It's a good word — something between *squirm* and *flinch*. The word illustrates the uneasy silence that is often attached to this chapter of our lives.

Even though there are roughly tens of thousands of books about menopause, it still lacks enough good stories. Much of the existing literature is clinical, offering women definitions, lists of symptoms, and possible treatments. This book is different. It is not about what menopause is, but about how it feels. As Donna Caruso writes, "Spare me the lecture on the righteousness of the cycle of life." There will be none of that in these pages.

Instead, we searched for stories that we wanted to read, that were beautifully told, and reflected our experiences and the experiences of people we knew. Our contributors offered us cultural references like Chrissie Hynde, Tori Amos, Billy Idol, and Lemony Snicket. They countered the cliché that menopausal women are all used up and instead gave us vitality, creativity, sexual craving, and lust. And they offered us points of views and perspectives that went beyond women. Menopause is experienced by non-binary people and trans men too.

Our call for submissions brought us a huge variety of literary forms as well. The anthology includes stories, poems, creative

1

non-fiction, a dramatic monologue, two interviews, a poem with a provocative prose introduction, a poem in two languages, and a list of facts and fictions about menopause. All of these add depth to the collection and an understanding that there are different ways of seeing and reading experience.

Within these pages are brains and bodies both lamenting their losses and eager to see what is next. The menopause experience is not simply something to survive. Unburdened by childbearing expectations and, possibly, by other gendered ways of under-standing themselves, those in menopause climb mountains, take on lovers, create art, daydream, undertake scientific explorations, and transform themselves with an urgency that springs from the bittersweet realization that their time is short.

We divided the anthology into three parts, with titles meant to invoke contradiction and capture the multiplicity of the menopausal experience. There is no one way to think about or experience menopause, and, certainly, there is no right way. The first section, "un/done," includes works that describe a desire to be done with social and cultural constraint, and to challenge the cliché that menopause means life is over. The second part, "in/fertile," sometimes celebrates and sometimes mourns the end of reproductive fertility, while acknowledging a new kind of fertility that might, or might not, emerge. Finally, the third part, "un/known," contains works that capture the sense of being out in a new world, not knowing oneself, or, conversely, knowing oneself at last. These pieces find their characters revising what they thought they knew. Many of the pieces could have found a home in any of the three parts, a confounding problem for the editors, but one that speaks to the depth and complexity of experience that these works describe.

As editors, we have found joy, commiseration, and kinship in these pages. We hope readers will find this and more.

Now, let the squinching begin.

ONE: UN/DONE

The Chrissie Hynde Stories

REA TARVYDAS

#1

I sat in a barbershop in Calgary, Alberta. Chrissie Hynde was in the adjacent chair with her feet up on the counter. Her biker boots were scuffed, the soles worn. A minute earlier, the barber had refused to shave my head. I asked him why and waited. He ignored me and repeatedly dipped a comb in blue tonic. "You're great," he said in Chrissie Hynde's direction.

"No, I'm not great. I'm an ordinary person who plays in a band. Why won't you shave her head?"

"It's the easiest way to grow out the grey." I pushed my unruly hair behind my ears. There was an inch of grey at the roots.

The barber narrowed his eyes at me. "It's too short for a woman. Besides, I don't want to be responsible for someone who has her head shaved, then jumps off a bridge. No way." He was a big man with small, close-set eyes, and an oversized head. His hair was dyed black and carefully combed over a bald spot.

I assured him I would not throw myself off any bridge.

"Women your age—" The barber draped a towel across my nape.

"What's that supposed to mean?" I asked.

"That's misogynistic bullshit and you know it," said Chrissie Hynde.

The barber was silent, so she stood, grabbed a pair of scissors and set to trimming her bangs. The cuts were small but rough.

Effective. Those bangs framed her kohl-ringed eyes to perfection.

"Looks good," I said.

"It's always a mess but I've learned how to manage it. I'm pretty comfortable with my look." She wore a singlet under a blue vest, faded jeans and a black-and-white striped tie.

"You're not very feminine," said the barber. He snapped a nylon cape on me. Placed his hands on my shoulders like he wanted to calm himself down.

"Listen, I never wanted to be known as a girl in a band. I wanted to be known as a rock n' roll musician," said Chrissie Hynde.

And this got me thinking about how, the last few years, I wanted to be known not as a woman, but as a person. How I'd taken to wearing androgynous clothing and how I felt uniformly free.

"Shave it off," I told the barber. He complied.

#2

I travelled to The Banff Centre to work on a novel. I woke sick with strep throat. I was delirious by lunchtime. It was February and minus forty degrees Celsius. The windows were frosted over with a half inch of ice that was clawing up the glass like it wanted to escape. The in-house doctor prescribed antibiotics. I was put into quarantine, but twice a day I wandered over to the dining room and choked down a bowl of soup.

At lunchtime, the waitress leaned in and asked, "Have you seen the athletes?"

It hurt to shake my head.

"There are eight hundred athletes here for the Junior Olympics. We've got them billeted in the theatres out back. There are so many, we're feeding them in shifts."

"Haven't seen them," I whispered. My throat was shredded.

Later, in my room, my fever spiked and the walls started leaning in. Trails of colour rose from the TV. And I thought I could hear the athletes below, talking and laughing together on their way to dinner. Delirious, I shoved a chair to the window and climbed onto it. Balancing, with my fingertips on the metal transom, I could just see over the ice. The angle was acute. The walkway was empty. No athletes.

There was a knock at the door. It was Chrissie Hynde.

"Hey, how's it going?"

I told her about my throat.

"Throats. Listen, I know throats. You got a kettle? I'll make you a hot toddy." She held out a bottle of whisky.

I crawled into bed while Chrissie bustled around my room, clearing away my clothes and making space on the desk for a small box she had fished out of her messenger bag.

"What's in there?"

"Stuff from home. I've been on the road a lot. I know to put together a lotta things out of little Ziplocs."

"Have you seen the athletes?" I inhaled cinnamon bark fumes. They reminded me of my father and I hadn't thought about him in months. Dad swore by the efficacy of hot toddies. "Cures what ails you," he would say, and then plunk down a steaming mug of brown liquid.

"I don't know what you're talking about, sick girl," said Chrissie Hynde. So I explained.

"No athletes," she replied and spun in the office chair. Her hair was pulled into a messy ponytail and I could see a bit of grey at her temples.

After a while, she asked, "What are you writing?" And I tried to explain my amorphous novel. I'd grown scared of its size.

"The writing process. Ain't it grand? You'll get there."

Chrissie Hynde brewed another hot toddy, took a sip, hesitated, then said, "I have to tell you something. But you have to promise not to say anything to anyone."

I promised.

"I'm thinking of going out on my own. I'm writing a buncha new songs. I swore I'd never do it and here I am, going solo."

#3

I was standing among the avocados and blood oranges. Chrissie Hynde had shared her favourite salad recipe and I wanted to try it for dinner. A woman in her fifties stopped me and said, "You're too old to be out in public wearing those." And she pointed at my cargo shorts.

"Fuck off." It came out of my mouth before I could stop myself.

"That's not nice."

"You're not nice. I've never met you and you come up to me and tell me I shouldn't be seen in public wearing shorts."

"It's unseemly," said the woman. And I knew she was referring to my varicose veins.

"Fuck you," I said with no hesitation. Later, I e-mailed Chrissie Hynde to tell her about my experience in the produce department at Safeway. I got an automatic response that indicated she was out of the country.

#4

Transporting my completed novel manuscript, I rode an asphalt escalator across Southern Ontario. I came upon Chrissie Hynde. She was playing a solo gig in the middle of a farmer's field — empty save a small herd of cows grazing on cut hay.

"What are you doing?" I asked.

"I'm heading out on the road next month. I've gotta practice." She strapped on her guitar and bent over a piece of equipment. There was a howl of feedback that she hastily subdued. I stared at the herd, knots of black-and-white cows with broad backs.

"New songs?"

She nodded. "*Stockholm*'s the name of the album."

"Like Stockholm syndrome?"

"Nah. I went to Stockholm and recorded it there. But I know what the syndrome is. I mean, I read up on it."

And I remembered a recent trip to Florence. In the Uffizi gallery, immense Renaissance paintings leaned over me like darkness visible. I grew frightened and escaped to a concrete bench in the packed square. Later, at the business hotel, I dreamt I was choking on blood-red oil paint.

"Are you scared?" My lips dried as I recalled the oozing sensation of my dream.

"You better believe it. It's just me. No one else. I mean, a band has a personality of its own and once you know what it is, it's pretty comfortable up there on stage. What the hell. It's only failure." Chrissie Hynde tuned her guitar, then launched into a jangled riff. When the amp crackled, the cows took off on an awkward run.

#5

I moved house. That is, I lifted up my bungalow and moved it to Saskatchewan. I'd always wanted to live by the Qu'Appelle River and figured my old house would survive the long trip down the TransCanada Highway. An urbanite wanted my narrow city lot, but not my sturdy bungalow.

I drove the pilot pickup truck forty kilometres an hour across the flatlands while Chrissie Hynde rode shotgun. "WideLoad" flashed the pilot pickup as it inched ahead of the flatbed that carried my bungalow, warning drivers all the way to Saskatchewan. "WideLoad, WideLoad, WideLoad." That would be me. Too wide for places like city lots, office jobs, and marriage. Chrissie Hynde carried a red-and-white megaphone and, every once in a while, would announce a random thought out the open window.

"What happened with your husband?" she asked.

"I just need to be alone for a while." I needed time to figure myself out.

"Listen, I've been on my own for a long while. I didn't exactly plan on it happening. It just happened. But I believe in love."

And I told her how I didn't know what I believed. About a lot of things: writing, love, marriage. How living with a middle-aged man preoccupied with his aging body was hard work. How I couldn't talk to him. How I couldn't talk to strangers anymore.

"We're all strangers, aren't we?" she blasted through the megaphone.

I winced. "Do you have to use the megaphone?"

"You bet. I've got shit to say. Why in the hell are you moving your house, anyhow?"

"Geographical adventure. Dangerous impulses beneath the stucco."

"The wiring's hot?"

I nodded and fiddled with the radio knob. Reception was intermittent on that one stretch of road.

"Yeah, that's menopause for you. Listen, you gotta have fun. I had an affair with a younger man a few years ago," she blurted out the window through the megaphone. A chain of birds startled off the telephone wires that underlined the prairie sky.

"What was that like?"

9

"It was a doomed relationship, but the sex was fantastic. You're on hiatus from your marriage. You should give it a try."

I considered sex with a younger man. Twenty-five years since I'd disrobed in front of a man other than my husband. I considered the dangers of vigorous sex when lubrication was an issue. Cystitis at a minimum. "I don't think I'm ready for that."

"Do it anyway," said Chrissie Hynde. And she asked me to pull over. The last I saw of her was in the rear view. She was standing in the middle of the road outside of Moose Jaw. The megaphone remained.

Let's Talk About Sex

TARYN THOMSON

I don't want to talk about menopause. I want to talk about sex.

And not that perfunctory been-there-done-that-twelve-or-thirteen-quick-thrusts-before-sleep sex.

I want to talk about sex that makes vases on bedside tables crash and ooze water all over my library books. I want to talk about the kind of sex that makes me flush all over when I remember it, calling the encounter to mind often, days and days after. I want to talk about the kind of sex where I find myself on the floor and wonder "how did that happen?" as I breathe heavily in the sticky, dreamy luxury of post-Olympic coitus.

Correction.

I don't want to talk about this kind of sex. I want to have this kind of sex. Regularly. So I don't want to talk about menopause. Not now. Not ever.

Menopause — with its hot flashes and mood swings and vaginal dryness and spotting — Jesus. Haven't we been through enough? We've tackled PMS. We've given birth. We've had D and C's. We've allowed the regular pap smears. We have taken birth control pills that gave us headaches and blood clots. We have suffered through condoms and gels and foams that, it turns out, we are allergic to, so they burned us something awful. We have had abortions and miscarriages. Christ. We, and our entire female package, have gone the fucking distance.

I don't want to talk about menopause. Not now.

11

I am only just hitting my stride.

Being divorced, I get to try out new lovers periodically and each lover is another uncharted field to navigate. I am getting more and more experimental, more playful and hungry. And the wonderful thing about loving in my forties is my hang-ups are pretty much dealt with. I accept I have a belly and lines around my eyes and places on my body that jiggle as I walk away from him to go to the washroom. I also know I am a hot number.

Midlife crisis is a term we use to describe people who refuse to surrender. What is so wrong with still wanting adventure? With wanting more adventure than ever? With putting up a bit of a fight? I am in my mid-forties. I am not about to fucking slow down. I am just getting started.

Look, we have steered these bodies through a lot: through our twenties when we didn't know what we wanted or how to ask for it; through our thirties where we were primarily milking/mothering machines; into our forties where finally, finally we walk tall and know enough to stride away from things that don't serve us and confidently ask for what we actually need. True, we bear the marks of the journey. We are not as smooth as we once were. Our bodies have stretch marks and rolls and lines and squishy bits, but we have brought them through one hell of a tsunami and now we are strong enough and old enough, by God, to do what we like with them.

I don't have a problem with reality. I will get older and my body will fail and my looks will no longer be there and I will die. This is natural.

However, don't make me talk about menopause. I don't want to embrace it. I don't want to accept it. I want to fight it and I will. I plan to fuck my way right through my geriatric years.

Menopause. Jesus.

I am not going to talk about that.

Eating Beets During Menopause

DONNA CARUSO

Right from the jar with a fork I suck, beet juice dripping. I'm desperate for redness, want it on my tongue, inside me, outside me, paint for my warrior face, for my warrior place, addicted to those blood red days, drunk with missing those blood red days.

I smile meekly, polite as always, as if I'd been caught in some sinful pleasure of youth, some foolish pleasure of old age. The way it really is, there's a pack of dingoes inside me, teeth tearing like mad, craving red meat, red beets, red-blooded life.

My red trail marked my lovers, my babies, my fingerprints in blood, I have lived other lives when life grew inside me, but I die prematurely when bloodless menopause comes in the pale afternoon as I recline like a ghost, drained of colour, barren as a desert, seeking respite. Please pass the beets.

Nostalgia, yes; denial, yes; grieving, yes, yes, yes. Pour red wine where blood once flowed. Quicken my heart with red memories: sweet cherries, raspberries, red beets, a red tongue singing old-time songs of yesterdays when the moon beat the rhythm of life. Pass the beets, now, I howl.

When blood pulsed through plump veins, the flush of excitement that was my life thrilled me. Now, in retreat, my blood hides from me, my skin shrivels in the sunshine. Where once I was a gathering place for women, men, and children, I am alone. Don't talk to me about the wisdom of crones. Don't talk about the phases of the moon. Spare me the lecture on the righteousness of the cycle of life. Leave me my beets and memories, my blood red, howling red beets.

This is the rage of my present life: life is maddeningly calm. The maniacal hormonal surges have subsided. Where has passion slipped off to? Where the danger of bleeding in public? Where has the possibility of being pregnant after every coupling gone?

Feed me beets and make me bleed again so I might throb with the possibilities of life and death and know the luxury of my voice singing in triumph. Who can stand this calm? No wonder old ladies dye their hair blue! No wonder we strike out with our umbrellas! We are mad as corpses with the calm of a bloodless life.

Cover me with rose petals, red and fragrant; feed me beets and red red berries; tell me how I blush and flush and gush in gorgeous rednesses. Don't feed me watercress sandwiches and tea in the afternoon parlour; look at me! All my life I've been a warrior, fearless in the face of bleeding, a priestess on the sacred altars. I cannot stop!

I Found Her at the Beach

B. A. MARKUS

Photo Credit: Donna Shvil

It was a sunny day but she wasn't dressed for it. She said she was making art with her feet. Digging holes all over the beach on the south side by the stairs. And she wasn't alone. No, she had a whole flock of ladies with her. All clucking like hens about making those ugly holes and actually mad at me for not joining in. Like I was some kind of traitor. I told her in my opinion it wasn't art they were making. It was some kind of crazy menopausal mess. Just hormones.

She didn't like that. She said they were using the sand and their feet to make a giant vagina or some such thing. She said they were trying to get the attention of the Prime Minister. Make him protect the oceans. From the oil tankers and pipelines. And from other opportunities that build the economy and give people jobs.

But I'll tell you this, just looking at that thing made me sick to my stomach. Everyone knows you can't make anything with your feet. A bunch of old ladies can't make art. And I can tell you one thing for sure, the kind of people who make giant sculptures of vaginas out of sand with their feet are exactly the kind of people the Prime Minister is never going to listen to. Imagine thinking anybody would care what old women like us have to say.

In Charge

GLENDA BARRETT

After I grieved
the empty nest twice,
my body signalled the end
of my childbearing days.
My life changed from
diaper days, lost sleep,
chicken pox, and measles
to night sweats and mood swings.

Who am I now? I wondered.
It had always been about others.
Now, I was forced to take my turn.
I began to nurture my tired body
and it soaked it up like a sponge.
Before long, everything changed.
For the first time in thirty years,
I found myself saying these words,

I'll be in charge of my life now.

Caged

LORI D. ROADHOUSE

Female gorilla holds aloft the knife
accidentally dropped into her enclosure.
Eyes him warily. She knows what he wants.
"Get the fuck away from me, Silverback!"

"Hey, hey we're the monkeys, we just monkey around!"
She glares at him, bares her teeth. Hisses, even.
She's tired of this cage, tired of the judgemental,
gawping gawkers filing by. Wants out.

This was for better or worse, but not for this.
Not for a lifetime of hell-in-a-cage.
She drops the knife with a clatter, panting and
sweating, head down, clings to the bars. She's rattled,

weary of making waves, weary from making babies.
She knows his shtick. She heard it through the
grapevine he's been swinging on in his spare time.
He and that new gal from Boston. Yes, she

heard about their funky monkeying around
and no, she's not going bananas.
She needs out. Out. Damn spot she's in.
"An increasing number of marital deaths are

a symptom of underlying marital woes."
She read that in the paper this morning, during
her last hormone-induced personal sauna.
The knife incident wasn't truly an accident in

this series of unfortunate events. Tell that to
Lemony Snicket. It'd knock his balls out of the wicket.
A ticket wicket. "Buy me a ticket on the last train
anywhere but home tonight."

She picks up the knife from the kitchen sink,
where it had fallen with a clatter.
Hot flash over, she resumes, resigned,
peeling the potatoes for his dinner.

Dervish

SALLY ITO

Grumble puss and consternation, maudlin matron is at the helm,
tears like crumbs at the plate's edge, running down
the dry cheeks' plain of daily existence—
that pored, age-spotted prairie—skin's chagrin at getting old.
Something and everything frustrates—lost mittens by kittens,
the What's-for-Supper? madness of ravenous crow-haired teen,
the I-can't-find-it look of the husband
who probably wants something younger, more tender, more juicy
than the hunk of flesh you slap on the plate for him.

Servitude no longer suits.
Submission is the will you have no stomach for.
You enter the Pause like a dervish
about to set fire to the wick of longing,
the hunger that has not been met
by your burrowing away of idylls and reveries you call poetry,
when all the words do is gasp and start
like a choked engine, sputterings out of the throat.

Disassembly

JANE CAWTHORNE

When the dog started coming around, I begged to keep him. I was eight years old and couldn't resist his wiry fur and one perked up ear. He was a dog who would listen to your problems or run eight miles in a snowstorm to get help if you busted your leg. He was a dog who could have had his own TV show. Dad wouldn't let us keep him. He said we couldn't afford a pet and, anyway, animals were for working or for eating. But we all knew the dog only kept coming around because Dad was feeding him scraps.

After a month or two, Mom gave him a collar. Dad came into the kitchen while Mom was drying the dishes and held the collar up in front of her like he was presenting evidence to a jury. "Was this you?"

"Yes."

"Strays don't have collars."

"It's not a stray. You feed it every day. Danny walks it."

I didn't want to get into trouble. "No I don't. It just follows me. I can't help that."

Mom shook her head and stacked the last of the plates back inside the cupboard.

"You women are always trying to domesticate everything. Let the dog be. Danny, stop walking the dog. It's not yours."

But with winter coming, Dad made a swinging door into the garage and left an old plaid sleeping bag on the cement floor so the dog wouldn't be cold. I bought him treats from my birthday money and named him Buddy, but I was the only one who called him Buddy. Everyone else called him "the dog."

Dad worked on the disassembly line at the Hanover slaughter-house. Any kid in town could tell you what happened to a cow once it went into the chute. First, it got shot in the head with a stun gun. Then it got hooked up to an overhead track by its hind legs and flipped upside down. Next, the throat got slit. The blood drained out and went through a grate and into a trough that ran the length of the line. After that, the hide got peeled back from the neck. Dad did the next job, which was to cut the cow straight down the centre of the belly and pull its innards out. If he nicked the intestines, he would contaminate the whole carcass. Guys got fired for that. But Dad was good with a knife. Fast. Precise. Once it was eviscerated, the carcass got split in half down the centre of the backbone, and the pieces got smaller and smaller until they were nice and neat and bloodless, wrapped in cellophane and ready for a supermarket shelf.

"Thank God for the all the crazy shapes and sizes of cows," Dad used to say, "If it weren't for that, we'd all be replaced by robots. That's job security."

Mom never said slaughterhouse. She called Dad's work an abattoir. She was different from the other moms we knew. She was from Toronto. She played piano. After school, I'd come home to the smell of pot roast from the kitchen and the sound of a sonata from the living room. She played Chopin, Liszt, Schubert, and Mozart, studying the sheet music and making notations. Sometimes she would play the same eight or ten measures a hundred times in a row, her wrists high, her thin fingers flying over the keys. When she was like this she was lost to us. My brothers and I could come home with bloody noses and she wouldn't notice. Mom's parents had expected her to go to the Royal Conservatory of Music in Toronto and become the wife of an architect, lawyer, or doctor. After she and Dad eloped, her parents sent her their baby grand piano. Mom called that "a gesture." Every year or two, they would send Mom a train ticket and she would visit them. She always went alone. To me, her parents were a photograph in a drawer. That was before we went to live with them after everything happened with the dog.

Even if it was only a baby grand, we probably had the only grand piano for a thousand miles. It took up three quarters of the living room. Mom polished it to a mirror finish once a week, and every spring she would call the piano tuner to undo the damage caused by the dry prairie winter. She treated the piano tuner with the deference usually reserved for a doctor, and she would guide him by the elbow from the door to the piano. For as long as I could remember, he would come in the spring and place his white cane against the low notes of the keyboard, sit down and play a few runs, and then make "tsk" sounds for an hour or so as he worked.

The piano tuner was like no other man I had ever seen. He always wore a suit and tie and smelled like soap and ironing. He was thin and straight backed and used to take my hand and hold it for a minute when he visited. He didn't shake it; he held it, sometimes putting it between both of his hands and giving it a little squeeze. When I was about five, he asked me when I was going to start to play. I didn't know what to say, but after he left, I ran my fingers up and down the keys careful not to press any. Mom hated it if we goofed around at the piano. That night, Mom told us the piano tuner had once played Carnegie Hall.

"What's Carnegie Hall?" I asked.

Andrew punched my leg and I yelped.

Dad swatted the back of Keith's head. "Don't hit your brother."

"It wasn't me!"

"That's enough." Mom told us about big concerts she had been to in Toronto and I forgot how much my leg smarted. She asked me, "Would you like to learn? You'd have to study very hard to be as good as the piano tuner."

Keith sneered. "Piano is for girls."

"Not true," said Mom. "Look at Liberace."

Andrew and Keith howled. Dad tried not to laugh and Mom scowled at him.

Dad pulled himself together. "Your long-suffering mother has had five sons and finally one is interested in the piano. If Danny wants to learn to play, there's nothing wrong with that."

Mom got up and patted Dad on the shoulder. "That's right. We'll start lessons. Twice a week after school, Tuesday and Thursday."

Keith mouthed, "Mama's boy." I stuck my tongue out and Dad cuffed me on the side of the head, but that didn't wipe the smile from my face. After dinner, Mom got out the special ice pack she had made for Dad's cutting hand, slipped it on him like a mitten and kissed him on the forehead.

Dad said, "Play something for me."

That was when they were still in love.

I never did set foot in the slaughterhouse. I had heard too many of Dad's stories. Men got knocked over by swinging carcasses and fell into the blood and slop. Sometimes the stun gun wasn't positioned quite right or the cow bolted, and it was still alive and flailing when it got flipped upside down. My brothers begged for details. They wanted all the gore, wanted to know how a guy's arm looked when he accidentally slashed it open, if Dad had seen any bone and how many stitches it took to close up the cut.

I was haunted by the idea of human blood mixing with cow blood, the stench of cow shit and innards, and the sound it must have made when it slopped into the channel below the floor. I remember asking, "What happens to all the blood?" and my brothers went crazy-eyed. They said it got put into tomato juice and ketchup. Mom told them not to give me ideas. She told me not to worry. But she never did tell me where the blood went.

Maybe I was a Mama's boy. Nobody paid much attention to Mom but me. I was the last to leave in the morning and the first to get home after school. Dad worked late on union business. He was the shop steward and carried a lot of weight in town. My oldest brother Brian worked at the farm supply and lived in an apartment above the store. Frank was in the army training to be a pilot. My twin brothers, Andrew and Keith, were in grade eleven and pretty much lived for the football team. And then there was me. The surprise baby. Andrew and Keith told me that Mom had really wanted a girl.

Some days, I would get home from school and she would be on the couch, an electric fan pointed right at her and the windows open even if it was snowing out. Or I would find her in the kitchen mopping her face with the hem of her apron, or sitting at the table with her head in her hands. She cried often.

One day, she was lying on the couch again with her arm folded across her eyes and said, "Danny, you know how to get a hold of your father? If something happens to me?"

"What's going to happen to you?" I felt my panic rise and I wanted to run for the phone.

Mom moved her arm from her eyes. "Forget it. Everything's fine. I'm fine." But when she stood up, there was a big crimson stain on the damask couch cushion. I couldn't breathe. I pointed at the couch and her hands flew to the back of her skirt. "Oh, for the love of Pete."

"Should I get Dad?"

"It's nothing. Go outside."

But it wasn't nothing. I grabbed my bike and rode as fast as I could to the farm supply. When I found Brian, I told him what had happened. He blushed and told me to lower my voice. He told me it was just woman stuff. He said everyone's mother went through it. He said not to tell anyone else and that Mom needed her privacy.

"But the blood."

"Trust me. Don't worry about it."

How could I not worry? When I got back, I went straight to the couch and checked the cushion. It was turned over, still wet underneath, but the blood was gone, and Mom was wearing a different skirt.

"Mom?" I needed to know if she would die.

"Everything's fine, dear. Please don't mention it to your father. And stay off the couch."

That was when things started to fall apart.

Dad was late that night. By the time he came in, we had almost finished dinner. He went to the fridge, grabbed a beer and brought it to the table. "Sorry I'm late. Had to fill out an accident report. New guy lost three fingers this morning. We only found one.

Don't buy ground beef for a while." He said this lightly like a joke, but we could tell by the look on his face and the tightness of his jaw that it wasn't funny.

I stared at my last bit of sausage. For once, the twins didn't ask for details. We kept quiet and waited for Dad to say more. We knew he had a lot on his mind and although he always told us it wasn't our business, I always felt like it was.

In a while he said, "We told them the line's moving too goddamn fast."

"Dennis, please. The children." Andrew and Keith shot each other a crooked half-smile. Mom put her knife and fork down and pushed her plate away. "Let me get you a glass."

"Don't bother." He massaged his wrist.

Mom stood. "Your ice pack."

"Doesn't help. Just get me the damn pills. They're going to bust the union. You mark my words."

Mom skirted around him to the cupboard and came back to the table with his pills. He tilted his head back and swallowed them, washing them down with beer.

"I'm calling the piano tuner this week," Mom said, trying to change the subject.

Dad put his beer bottle down. "You know we can't afford it."

"But, we do it every—"

"The piano sounds fine to me."

"Would you let the car go without service?"

Andrew's and Keith's eyebrows shot up. Mom hardly ever talked back to Dad.

"That racket when it idles isn't the sound of a car that's seen a mechanic lately."

"I could teach a few piano lessons."

"We're fine."

Mom kept going. I was thrilled but terrified too. "I'd be grateful for something to do. I've got time on my hands."

"You've got Danny to teach."

Everyone looked at me like I'd done something wrong.

"It's not like I'd be working," said Mom. "It's just lessons."

Dad pushed away his meal and said, "I'm done," and headed out the mudroom door to the garage. We heard the dog bark.

Andrew and Keith took their plates to the sink without being asked. I fell asleep that night to the sound of Dad chopping wood in the yard.

The next morning after Dad left for work, Mom smoothed her apron over her skirt, picked up the phone and made an appointment with the piano tuner for the end of June. The twins looked up from their Wheaties.

"It's none of your business," she said.

By the end of the week, Mom had five students. She arranged for them to come after school and be gone well before Dad got home. The secret didn't keep for long. On Friday, Dad stormed in after work and demanded to know if what he had heard was true.

"Lessons, Ruth? I said clear as day I was against it."

Mom squared her shoulders. "I can't cancel now. I've promised to teach until summer holidays."

Dad left the house without saying a word. Mom shrugged her shoulders at me. "Don't worry. He'll come around. He always does."

But he didn't. Dad started missing dinner. He'd come home late smelling like the bar and then stay out in the garage until he went to bed. At nine o'clock one night, Mom sighed and sent me out with a plate of meatloaf, potatoes, and canned peas. As I approached the garage door, I heard him talking to Buddy. "What else could I do? I would have lost my job." The dog was listening, one ear up, head tilted, with deep understanding on his face. Buddy heard me approach and tilted his head my way. I coughed and Dad turned. He saw the plate and grumbled something. I set it on the workbench.

"What happened, Dad?"

"Fletcher and Bouchard got laid off."

They were men who lived on our street.

When I went inside and told Mom, she sent me back out with some apple crisp and a soup bone.

At the beginning of May, Dad lost his job too. Janice Kopecki's dad drove his cop car up our driveway. Mom was waiting. It was like she already knew.

It was four in the afternoon, but Dad stumbled out of the back seat and Mr. Kopecki tipped his hat. "They called the station from Jack's and I said I'd go get him. He's all right. Give him some coffee."

Mom saw him to the kitchen where he slumped in a chair. She said, "Danny, go up to the high school and see what Andrew and Keith are doing."

I sat on the floor in the mudroom, put my sneakers on slowly and pretended to be invisible. Dad's eyes were bloodshot, rimmed red and watery. "Twenty-four years. Where's the loyalty? They won't say it, but I know why. Top of the pay scale. They hire these goddamn immigrants who'll work for nothing and don't even know that they're being taken advantage of." Mom reached for the coffee pot but dad shook his head and said, "Just the pills." He put his head down on his arms. "Ruth, I don't know how to do anything else."

Mom put her hand on his shoulder. He kept his head down. She went back into the cupboard and brought down a Chock Full o' Nuts tin. She pulled money out and laid the bills on the table in front of him. "Here, I can help. It's from the lessons." Her face was beaming.

Dad pushed the money away, got up, knocked his chair over and stormed past me on his way to the garage. He didn't even look at me. Mom yelled after him, "Pride goeth before the fall." She pushed the bills back in the can and put it away. I was still in the mudroom, afraid to move, trapped between Mom in the kitchen and Dad in the garage.

Over the next few weeks, Andrew and Keith showed up only to eat and sleep. Mom took on more students. Dad drank beer in the garage. Dinner was a minefield. We kept our heads down, ate in silence and asked to be excused as fast as we could.

Then one night as we were finishing our last few bites, Dad made an announcement. "I'm putting an ad in the paper tomorrow for the piano."

Mom's fork clattered off her plate to the floor. When I bent down to pick it up, my heart pounded in my ears.

"Why would you do that?" Mom's voice was cold.

"It's worth a few thousand. Enough to tide us over until I get some work."

"But it's our only source of income."

Dad banged his fist. "I've made my decision."

Mom put her napkin down, stood and said, "The piano is not yours to sell."

"It was a wedding gift. They gave it to both of us."

Andrew tugged my arm, a signal for me to leave the room with him and Keith.

From the hallway, I heard Mom say, "No. It came from my parents. They gave it to me. Me alone." I had never heard that voice before. She knew she was right, but the tremor in her words was full of fear and pain. I hated Dad for making her talk like that. No good would come of it. I wanted to be big, so I could be out of the house all the time like my brothers. What was happening didn't have anything to do with me and I wished I didn't know about it.

We heard the table squeak across the floor. "I won't have this, Ruth. I won't."

"Neither will I."

A plate crashed and the back door slammed. The dog barked. Then we heard Mom crying. Keith and Andrew pulled me into their room and they let me look at their comic books. I stayed with them until bedtime when I snuck back into the kitchen to see if there was anyone to say goodnight to. Mom was sitting at the piano, not playing, her wrists limp, her fingers still on the keys.

I try to remember the last time I actually spoke to my Dad and what it was I said. It's funny how when you don't know you're doing something for the last time, you don't pay attention to it. Maybe I said, "Please pass the salt." I don't know.

A week before summer vacation, I came home to a sign on the front door in Mom's handwriting apologizing that piano lessons were cancelled. The front door was locked. I ran around to the back and into the kitchen. Mom was standing at the counter with the phone in her hand, staring at the dial. Her eyes were puffy and red. She was sweating and fanning her face as if she might faint. I was sure the piano was gone, sure that Dad had sold it.

"How could he do it?" I ran toward the living room.

"Danny. Don't—"

I slipped past her before she could stop me. The piano was still there. I was so relieved I didn't realize what had happened right away.

From the doorway I heard Mom say, "He didn't mean it."

I walked toward the keyboard gingerly, half-terrified like I was approaching a wounded animal. An axe was sticking out of it, obliterating middle B, C, C# and D.

"What happened?"

Mom sobbed. "Oh Danny, I'm sorry. The piano tuner came. Your father was furious. I never should have called him. It's my fault."

"Where's the piano tuner?"

"Gone home."

My stomach went funny. "Is he okay?"

"Yes. He's fine. We're all just shaken up."

"Where's Dad?"

"I don't know." She leaned against the doorframe, put her face in her apron and wiped her eyes. When she took her hands away, she had arranged her face to be almost normal.

"What's going to happen?" I remembered the phone in her hand. "Who were you calling?"

"I couldn't decide."

Andrew and Keith came in then, breathless from running. Keith sat down at the kitchen table. "This is some crazy day. Can I have a sandwich?"

Mom got out the cheese and bread. "What are you doing home so early?"

Andrew said, "Practice is cancelled. Didn't you hear?"

Mom glanced toward me in the living room. "Sit down with your brother, Andrew. I've got something to tell you." Keith leaned onto the back legs of his chair. Mom scolded. "Don't. You'll break it." Andrew snickered, grabbed a slice of cheese, peeled the plastic off, folded it in three and stuffed it into his mouth. "Andrew, wait till I make sandwiches. Please. Be civilized."

"The sirens went off and everything. The plant's shut down."

Mom stood motionless with the bread bag in her hand. "What are you talking about?"

Keith said, "Some maniac butchered a dog at the plant."

Mom dropped the bread.

"Yeah. He walked in with a dog. A dog! Hooked him up by his hind legs and everything." Keith made a slicing motion across his neck. "Someone on the line tackled the guy just as he was pulling the guts out. Cops are there. I heard they shot the guy."

Andrew said, "They did not. They're taking him to jail. Probably going to send him to the loony bin."

Keith leaned way back in his chair again. "I wonder who it was?"

The bile rose in my throat.

Mom's eyes narrowed. "Danny, go find the dog."

I didn't move.

Adjusting the Ashes

SUSAN CALDER

Rick's hand slides under her nightie and strokes her thigh. His body curls around hers, spoon-style. Carol shrugs her husband off. He rolls over and starts snoring. The bedside clock reads four a.m. Perimenopause, the doctor says, is making her restless. If it worsens, he'll prescribe pills. Carol slips out of bed. Rick shudders and returns to his deep, even breathing.

She tiptoes downstairs. Her nostrils prickle at the fresh paint smell. In the den, she turns on the desk lamp, illuminating the birthday cards on the window ledge. She picks up the one from her younger daughter, away at university.

WHAT'S SO GREAT ABOUT TURNING FIFTY?

She opens the card.

NOTHING.

Ha. Ha. She returns the card to the ledge. Might as well use these lost hours for work. At her desk, she opens her computer to review the Ashe file.

Harvey Ashe swallowed a mouse in his beer. Or so he alleges. His nuisance claim against the brewery Carol's company insures is worth three thousand dollars, tops. Instead of settling quickly, the novice adjuster had dithered. If she retains a lawyer, the company could face demands for lost wages, uninsured medical expenses, and pain and suffering totalling a quarter million dollars. She hopes she's taken over the claim in time for damage control.

She logs Ashe's address into her GPS and reaches for the

handcrafted card from her girlfriend, Patti. Last fall, Patti chucked her Calgary oil company job and drove to Yellowknife, NWT. What she's doing up there isn't clear.

"Stuff," Patti says when Carol asks.

"What stuff?" Nice to be single and do whatever the hell you want.

"The scenery is amazing. Sky like you wouldn't believe. Come up and see it some time."

On the front of the card, Patti drew a girl with long hair, sitting cross-legged on an empty road, one hand resting on a backpack, the other hand raised, thumb up. Above the sketch she printed: *Carol Before*. A depiction of their hitchhiking trip from Calgary to Newfoundland, thirty summers ago. The card's inside page contains only the words: *Carol After?*

Carol Between would be the years of normal, adult life. Marriage to Rick. Mother of two children. Insurance adjuster promoted to claims manager.

She sneezes. Rick's renovations haven't reached the den yet, but the dust has penetrated the whole house. His next project, now that both daughters have moved out, is to turn the cubbyhole rooms upstairs into a master bedroom loft. Another sneeze. Carol grabs a Kleenex. She shouldn't gripe about the dust. Ripping their house apart keeps Rick occupied since his company bridged him to early retirement. No doubt she'll enjoy their updated rooms if he ever gets around to finishing them.

Meanwhile, she's eager to meet Harvey Ashe this afternoon. In management, she misses the daily head-to-head dealings with claimants, unscrupulous or sympathetic. Does Ashe have plans for his insurance windfall? Given his machinist's income, he must be viewing this bottled mouse as a winning lottery ticket.

A HandiBus rumbles past Harvey Ashe's house, which looks in desperate need of new siding. Carol clacks up the sidewalk and uneven front steps. If she falls, she'll file a countersuit against the Ashes. She scans the chipped paint for a doorbell. This is the porch where the mouse-swallowing incident occurred. On that warm August evening, Ashe and his son-in-law brought beers out here, planning to relax.

With her knock, the door jerks open. A short man appears.

"Mr. Ashe?" She extends her hand.

His palm is velvety and delicate. Harvey Ashe's bald head lines up with her nose. He wears a checked shirt tucked into his jeans and a belt buckle decorated with a swirling *H.A.*

She follows him through the entrance cluttered with shoes and cowboy boots to the living room. A sofa, draped with a mauve throw, faces the front window and console TV. In the far corner, there's an armchair covered with a pumpkin and rust afghan. An upright piano stands against the wall.

It's only on second glance that Carol notices the lady on the La-Z-Boy chair by the doorway. Her hair is wispy, white. A shawl encloses her narrow shoulders. This can't be Mrs. Ashe. According to the reports, she is only sixty, ten years older than Carol.

Mr. Ashe introduces his wife, Bertha. "Call me Harvey," he tells Carol. "Can I get you coffee? Tea? Juice?"

"A glass of water is fine." She edges toward the sofa. The wall behind it is covered with children's portraits. "You have a large family."

Bertha's eyes water. She blinks.

Carol raises her voice. "Are those all your—?"

"We have three children." Bertha's voice is deep and startlingly clear. "Some of the pictures are of the grandkids."

Carol lays her briefcase on the sofa. "Nice-looking bunch."

Trite but true. Their skin tones range from freckled snow to teak, their hair shades from platinum to carrot to raven. Harvey's face has the ruddiness common to redheads.

Carol slides her fingernail into the throw's crocheted spider-web weave. "Did you make this?"

Bertha nods and cranks the recliner footrest, propping up her scuffed slipper soles. Harvey returns with a tray topped with two glasses of water, a glass of orange juice, and a plate of oatmeal cookies. He sets the tray on the coffee table and crosses the room to the armchair.

Carol sinks into the sofa, moves to the highest cushion, but still looks up at both claimants. Not a strong bargaining position.

After she and Harvey chat about this year's unusually hot July weather, Carol suggests he begin by recounting his experience. "I don't suppose you like remembering," she adds to show support.

"It don't bother me to talk of it." Harvey's glance passes from his wife to the porch visible through the window. "It was almost a year ago. Last August, me and Tareq — that's my daughter's husband — spent the day repairing the back patio. By afternoon, we were sweating. We got some cold ones from the fridge and went out to the shaded front porch. The beer tasted good and was going down easy."

She picks up her pen and steno pad to take notes in case Harvey contradicts his original statement.

"All of a sudden, something solid hit my tongue," he says. "I tried to spit, you know, by reflex. Part of it slithered down my throat."

Carol shudders. "Part?"

Harvey looks at Bertha. "The mouse's top end went down. The backside hung from my mouth. Its tail tickled my chin. I watched the butt disintegrate and yanked the tail. That creature was brewed, most likely caught in a vat, but I grew up on a farm and know a mouse's hindquarters when I seen it."

Her hand goes weak, but she manages to keep scribbling.

"I held the remains up to Tareq." Harvey raises his left hand, his fine fingers mimicking the action. "I dangled it back and forth. Tareq says, 'That'll teach you not to drink so much, Dad.' And you know that mouse put me off beer for a solid month, which wasn't such a terrible thing." He pats the buckle on his slim waist.

"That's why you didn't report the claim immediately?"

Harvey nods. "I figured I'd eaten worse. Us kids used to roast gophers, so what's the difference?"

"I wouldn't care much for gopher."

"Neither does Bertha, but I forgot that and carried the mouse into the kitchen, figuring she and my daughter would get a kick out of it. At first they thought it was a piece of string, but I explained." Harvey pauses for a drink of water. "Bertha backed into the sink. My daughter said, 'Dad, throw that disgusting thing in the trash — not under the sink — out in the lane.' Which I did, destroying the evidence, your adjuster who visited us says. At the time, I didn't think."

Harvey finishes his water. Carol's mind drifts to the summer she and Rick rented a cottage at Mara Lake, when their daughters were little. Patti and her then boyfriend came for a few days. While the men were out somewhere, a bat flew down the chimney into the wood stove. Carol scurried out of the kitchen. Patti thrust a badminton racket into the stove, scooped out the bat and circled the racket toward the shrieking kids. Carol had forced herself to peek at the sooty, winged rat.

She wriggles her shoulders to brush off the recollection. The steno pad is on the coffee table where she placed it. "Wouldn't a dead mouse be bloated from the brewing process and, when you tipped the beer back to drink, lodge in the bottle neck?"

"You'd think so." Harvey gets up. "Must have been a baby. Starting to decompose."

Carol fumbles for a water glass. Harvey offers her the cookie plate. She shakes her head. He holds out the orange juice to Bertha, who recoils into the recliner. The son-in-law's statement in the report jibed with Harvey's, which it would if the Ashes are good scammers.

Harvey takes two cookies for himself and returns to his chair. "The day after I ate it, I figured Bertha was joking when she jumped away from me and said, 'Don't touch me with that thing inside you.' I laughed, but Bertha knows a mouse's head is meat and would be absorbed into my system, instead of passing clear through me, like a penny, for instance." He munches a cookie while his wife cranks down the La-Z-Boy footrest. "Bertha started sleeping in my daughter's bedroom and a few months later couldn't drag herself to work. Our doctor sent her to a psychologist. He's tried everything — pills, different therapies. It's all in your reports."

Bertha's shrink concluded that her husband's mouse swallowing triggered a childhood trauma too buried for therapy to reach. The resulting depression forced her to quit her factory job five years short of retirement. In addition to lost income, there would be a reduced pension.

Carol turns to Bertha. "I understand you're also unable to do housework?"

Bertha rises. Her shawl slips down her fleece top.

"I don't mind handling those chores." Harvey mumbles while chewing. "Washing dishes and clothes and such gives me something to do. I lost my job this past winter."

"You were laid off?"

Bertha shuffles from the room.

"It wasn't mouse related," Harvey says. "Just a normal downsizing."

Such honesty would impress a judge or jury, if the case went to court. Most claimants would try to link the rodent swallowing to the layoff. With both spouses unemployed, a lawyer would add substantial figures for lost medical and dental benefits.

Harvey glances down the hallway, runs his index finger up his empty glass. "For me, the main problem is losing Bertha. I don't care particularly about her cooking and paycheque. I expect Bertha misses her music and crochet." His finger rests on the glass rim. "But for me, it's her looking over and smiling while she mashes potatoes for dinner. Us going for walks up the hill to see the sunset. Sleeping together, her crowding my side of the bed." Harvey pauses. His finger circles the rim. "About the bed—"

Loss of consortium, the lawyer would add to Harvey's claim. Carol notes this on the steno pad, wondering how much consorting is normal for a couple their age. A couple not much older than her and Rick, who haven't consorted for several weeks, and when was the last time she did it with genuine interest?

"By bed," Harvey says, "I don't mean so much the excitement, although that was always good." His expression softens as he stares at the vacant recliner chair. "I mainly liked being with her. You know?"

I don't know, at least I haven't known in years, Carol thinks as she drives past downtown towers. Why stop at her office to process claims that will only re-emerge in new form tomorrow and the day after that until she retires. Or, like her husband and Harvey Ashe, is declared redundant. She crosses the bridge to her neighbourhood, enters her lane and bumps over gravel to the shed Rick plans to replace with a double garage. In their backyard, she treads the paving stones that bisect the re-sodded grass. A year from now, the path will lead to a terraced deck, but today she takes a giant step up to the kitchen.

"Rick?" she calls.

Silence. He must be out, probably shopping for supplies for the upstairs renovations. She removes her high heels, pads from cool ceramic tile to living room hardwood to worn Berber carpet, plunks her briefcase on the den desk and sneezes. She squints at the window. Will they ever be rid of sawdust hanging in sunbeams? She closes the Venetian blind, stopping it halfway so it doesn't jostle the birthday cards. The blind slips; a corner nudges a card. It wavers and falls onto Patti's card, which knocks down the next and the next.

She tries to right the cards. They keep tumbling. Shit. The hell with them all.

Turning fifty is crap, but at least she still has a job, one she's good at. She opens her laptop to the Ashe file. What can she reasonably settle the claim for?

She calculates figures for lost wages, lost pension, and lost dental and medical benefits, and adds amounts for pain and suffering and loss of consortium. The total stares out at her from the computer screen, way too much for what should have been a nuisance claim. She pictures Bertha shuffling from her chair.

Carol adds an extra five thousand for pain, suffering, and loss. The number is ridiculous. If she recommends this to the company, the vice-presidents will freak.

Although, she could insist it's the minimum the Ashes will accept before consulting a lawyer. With her twenty-eight years in the business, the VPs would believe her.

Noise rumbles from the street. She pushes the blind up. Her husband's van draws to a stop at the curb. Rick gets out, goes to raise the tailgate, and yanks out plywood. He staggers as he adjusts the awkward load.

She reaches for Patti's birthday card. *Carol Before* hitches a ride on a highway. The breeze billows her hair. She opens the card. *Carol After?* She could tell Rick, "I need a vacation. We're not going anywhere this summer. I've never been to Yellowknife and Patti says the scenery's amazing."

Rick will say he'll miss her. He might feebly suggest he tag along. In the end, he'll appreciate not having her around so he can work like crazy creating the loft upstairs. Carol will go to Yellowknife alone.

She'll return to a revamped master bedroom.

Or not.

Long ago and far away

LOUISE CARSON

Long ago and far away
a woman trudged
with head bent into the storm
for of course snow was falling
and a cruel wind pressed it
into her face

long ago and far away
she felt silk slip to the floor
the oriental purple and gold pattern
she would know in her dreams
and there was only surprise
at the identity of the embracer
when she awoke although very little
surprise really only that there should
be more than one

night followed night
and they embraced her one after the other
all the refusals denials
even a few laughing
and she thought there
that's taken care of that
how easy how pleasant how relieved I am
to have finished acting.

Il y a longtemps

TRADUCTION PAR LISE TREMBLAY ET LOUISE CARSON

Il y a longtemps,
en des temps lointains.
Une femme marchait. Avec lassitude.
Sa tête pliait vers la tempête.
Bien sûr, il neigeait
et un vent cruel la prenait au visage.

Il y a longtemps,
en des temps lointains
elle sentit la soie,
glisser jusqu'au sol.
Le dessin oriental, de pourpre et d'or,
qu'elle voudrait dans ses rêves,
comme celui qu'elle embrasse,
et lorsqu'elle s'éveille
ce n'est pas très surprenant,
qu'il y en ai plus d'un.

Une nuit, puis une autre,
et ils l'embrassent, l'un après l'autre.
Tous les refus, les dénégations,
même certains souriants.
Et elle pensait : tiens donc !
Comme c'est facile,

comme c'est agréable,
quel soulagement,
j'ai fini de jouer.

woman burning

LYNDA MONAHAN

kick off the covers
fling my gown into the dark

I glow   am pure heat
the colour red
an element left on high

a white hot shiver I am
a lit cigarette smoking

your arm across my waist
is too heavy   too hot
your breath on my back
this room is a sauna

throw open the windows
I am a woman
burning up the night

Unzipped

MAROULA BLADES

Anne stops breathless on the frosty street ablaze with noise, conscious of herself rising to touch the sun midway up the dawn sky in all its greys, purples, and dusky pinks, loosely unfolding in the early stretch of day. Alone with the city's jagged contours and sharp turns stifling her walk, she hobbles forward, bereaved. Outside the self, it is a time of silence, a belly-aching spell. Age breaks through on all fours, bloated, howling below the skin like a mangy dog sweating in its fur.

"Age is a chisel," she thinks. "It digs and scrapes, filing away at life. Heat pulsates, flushing the flesh. Minus fifteen degrees and what hell is this sweat that trickles to what used to be the waistline and down the wide shoulders, chunky like my male cousin's shot-putter's back, oh God, the hurt and shame of it!"

Scorched by the second, blinded by the minute, fallen within an hour, friction crawls between her 113 kilos and the brown flannel clothing, chafing the skin. Anne tries to rise above the she-phantom now wriggling below her frame like a giant scarlet worm, its hunger insatiable. She shouts and cries, wanting to prise open every red vessel, summoning the waning will to rise and stake the beast and let her body breathe unhampered once more. Within moments she capitulates, falling brittle as chalk onto an orange brick wall, head spinning in a jungle of red and black carousels. She imagines that even the evergreen trees have taken on a psychedelic turn for the worse. Fuchsia leaves and yellow trunks. Green birds savagely pick at black nests. Eggs lie empty of yolks. The turf warps. Sunken to the core, Anne's nose drips, beads freeze around her blue-tinged mouth. She roughly rubs her face; tiny splinters of ice fall to her lap. Anne looks toward the iceblink in the distance with tears in her eyes and a belated prayer on her lips, as a soft voice patters in her mind, whispering:

"Embrace her to smooth the tidal dance below the skin. Each collision will rob you of breath if you don't kiss her cheek, now, quietly within the space of a turn. Let her know she is a part of you and you will both ride the incoming swell of a woman's change. So soft it can be, so soft within your reach."

Go. Rock.

NOAH MICHELSON: Last night, before you played "Ribbons Undone," you did a short improv about menopause.

TORI AMOS: A taboo subject.

NOAH: But one that you're not afraid of?

TORI: No. Not anymore. That changed in the last year.

NOAH: What happened?

TORI: Women have been talking to me about aging and being different ages — and all ages have been talking to me about the stresses of their particular age. I was working with Paule Constable — one of the great lighting designers — and Rae Smith — they worked on "War Horse" — and they were talking about the fact that [menopause] isn't discussed. I had *long* conversations with Rae, in stairwells, and with Paule, in the theater, and they would say to me, "You have to talk about it. You have to find a way to talk about it but in a way that makes it not about victimization." Ageism is a real thing. I had to get my head around how am I going to — in the music industry, be in front of the camera at fifty; it's not as if we — women — are seen as Johnny Depp and Brad Pitt where we're just coming into our hotness. They're leading men! There are leading women that are around my age, but it's just starting to happen. You're just starting to see that happen in the movie industry. But coming to a rock concert — [women] can't be doing granny rock. We're singing about emotions, we're singing about sexuality, we're singing about all these things. Whereas [there are] roles for Helen Mirren — who is the hottest thing I've ever seen — try and find her equivalent in rock and roll. We are having to carve that out for ourselves because you don't go see some of my contemporaries, you don't go see the Chilies [Red Hot Chili Peppers] and think *They need to be doing grandpa rock.* No! They're virile men who are sensual and they can sing about anything. Our culture doesn't see it that way [for women]. There are certain things, if you start singing about them — if you listen to the young girls, I hear them talk, "Oh! She looks desperate! That's so desperate!" Whether you're in your twenties looking desperate or you're in your fifties looking desperate — desperate is desperate. But you don't hear them say that about the guys! So, I needed to get my head around how I wanted to carve out the next fifty years. In order to grab it with both hands — to grab it! — I had to first go all the way into the projection from the culture.

NOAH: It felt like a part of the trajectory of what you've been involved in your entire life. [Your menopause improv] felt natural. The way you did it didn't seem like you were doing it to shock. I was surprised by it, but it made sense to me.

TORI: There's going to be more of that.

NOAH : There should be.

TORI: [*laughs*]

NOAH: But, because as you said, no one else is talking about this, do you feel an added pressure to take that on? Is this organic Tori Amos doing what she's going to do or is this you saying "I'm going to lead the menopausal charge"?

TORI: No. You have to be organic. [That improv] wasn't rehearsed. Not that something that's rehearsed can't be organic, I'm not saying that, but I think with the tour looming, I really don't know what it's going to be from night to night. There has to be a place where songs will come, conversations will happen.

NOAH: The thing that I loved about it was that you were making up this little song on the spot about needing your glasses and you didn't just sing about getting older, you used that specific word — menopause. And I think that's such a scary word for so many people and it conjures up very specific things: no longer being sexually virile, no longer being a woman — or at least being seen as useless in some ways in our culture. The fact that you went there—

TORI: In green leather pants... [*laughs*]

NOAH: In green leather pants no less! We don't ever see something like that. I'm *impressed*.

TORI: It's not an easy road. Menopause is a *tough* road and a *tough* teacher. Finding your own self-acceptance and sensuality within it is, well, sometimes it's a real hunt. You have to dive in there because of the feelings that you're having. All of the songs on this new record were written to deal with this stuff. There is a quiet, silent grieving that happens through menopause. It might happen in a way where you're not aware of it but you can begin to lose memory for a minute — you can forget things — and you're very aware that you're going through a different process, a different phase of life. Until you feel it and you're in it, you can't imagine what it is. Trust me — until those chemicals are happening in you, you don't know what that is. It's easy to sit and feel quite confident about yourself, *thinking* about how you're going to be in menopause, but that's not how it hits you.

NOAH: I believe it. As a thirty-five-year-old gay man, there are twenty-something-year-old gay guys who are ready to help me pick out my casket.

TORI: Yes. So, it becomes about how do you find empowerment through [aging]? That's been the reason I'm going out as a one-woman show. It's not because I don't love [my drummer and bass player] Matt [Chamberlin] and Jon [Evans], and it's not because I don't love the Polish quartet [that I toured with on my last tour], it's because my [thirteen-year-old] daughter Tash looked at me and said, "Okay, I get it. I get the fifty thing. I get that the frontline record deals at fifty and up are given more to men than to female singer-songwriters. What are you going to do, Mom? Because if you don't get your head around this, you're telling me that I've got nothing to look forward to when I'm fifty. What are you telling me? That that's it? Because the message is avoiding this at all costs and that's what you're telling me." And she said, "That's how you're going to deal with it?" And I said, "No." She said, "*Go. Rock.*" And the earth moved! And I looked in her eyes and it was real! There were tears in her eyes — "You've got to get this one, Mom, like you've never gotten anything else!" Because this is a demon. This is a *fucking demon*.

NOAH: That's not just empowering for your daughter, it's empowering for all of the people who have followed your work and who look to you as someone who is creating art that they find fulfilling and in some cases life changing. And I'm guessing the thought of you giving up that work is nothing short of devastating to a lot of people.

TORI: Menopause is a struggle. And it's a pejorative. I'm not here to try and make menopause sexy — that's not my message. My message is to feel empowered — and feel all these feelings while you happen to be going through menopause. It isn't sexy but *you* can be sexy. So look it in the eye.

NOAH: And don't let it defeat you.

TORI: That's right. So, okay, if I'm playing a show, whatever I'm wearing that night, I might break out in a hot flash during the show and it's not because of the lights. And what are we going to do? We're going to have towels on the side of the stage and we're going to fucking go with it. Because that's all we're going to do — there's no other answer. If it's going to be embarrassing, it's going to be embarrassing. But to get to that point, you can't think you're going to defeat it — I will forget the lyrics. I will have the wrong glasses because I'm not losing my mind — it's not early Alzheimer's — but other people going through it will say, these are the symptoms. You find ways to get through it. I have to take fifty by the hand — hold hands and welcome it with every cell and say, "Show me fifty like I didn't imagine." Not that other people aren't going through it, but show it to me in a way that *I* didn't understand. It's about asking fifty itself to open up my understanding, and then it's about just being alive — being truly alive!

Man with a Vagina

E. D. MORIN INTERVIEWS BUCK ANGEL

Buck Angel is a pioneering filmmaker, speaker and advocate. Born a biological female, he has conquered a lifetime of adversity to undergo his transformation into the healthy, happy, self-confident man he is today. The documentary about Buck Angel's life, *Mr. Angel*, was released to critical acclaim in 2013. Buck travels the world speaking and educating others.

E. D. MORIN: In the documentary film, *Mr. Angel*, you talk about having your first period and later about having a hysterectomy. At some point you must have had your last period. What was that like?

BUCK ANGEL: I remember exactly when I stopped having my period. Mostly because I just hated having it so much that I welcomed it the minute it stopped. It was the second month I was taking testosterone. My hormone doctor had no experience with trans men before me so he could not tell me when this would happen, so I wasn't expecting it to happen so fast. My period was always this thing that made me feel so female. I always would get so angry when it happened. I also had super bad cramping and just felt all-around horrible. So when it didn't come anymore I remember feeling like my life was changing.

E. D.: Do you identify with this particular change, menopause?

BUCK: Well I'm not sure if I actually identify with menopause but I think that it has happened to me. Men go through this change as well. I notice things that happen to me that could possibly be defined as menopause. Mostly when I am close to my next injection of testosterone. I usually feel a bit more moody or down. Not to say that is just what menopause is, but I think that the change in my body from the lack of the hormones is very similar to that of women. I also feel like after my hysterectomy I went through a type of menopause. I remember feeling very tired and not at my best, until I started to supplement with a DHEA [a steroid hormone] and get my estrogen levels back to normal. I think menopause is a real thing that many people in the trans world do not talk about.

E. D.: Do you think this reticence to talk about menopause in the trans world is coming from a place of identity?

BUCK: Yes, for sure because menopause has always been and still is associated with women. Trans men want to move as far away from that identity as possible. This is why I feel so passionate about discussing this from a male perspective. I think that if these guys can relate to it as male it will be easier for them to identify and thus work on how to improve on it.

E. D.: There's a menopause stigma for women too, despite all the books out there on the topic. Menopause is either a joke, or it begs immediate medical or therapeutic attention. There's no rational dialogue. That's why I think our stories are so important. We're not one thing. We're not our symptoms either. We're complex people. I think menopause messes with our identities in all sorts of ways. Do you think it's the same for the trans community? Maybe menopause, like so many other identity burdens, is something people in the trans world would love to eject from their lives. If so, I get that. Sometimes, as liberating as the end of all my periods is, I'd love to eject menopause from my life too!

BUCK: Well yes, we know that there is this stigma and like I said for trans men it seems to be the association with "female." It's such a difficult subject to discuss because of the negative history it has. I for one really feel the importance of bringing this out of that stigma and more into a situation that happens and is totally natural and normal. Since it has really never been something that men have discussed regarding their own health, I wonder if getting the conversation out there will break down that barrier and have men stop using it as a means of explaining why "women act this way."

E. D.: I admire your drive to redefine what is normal. It's a theme that comes up in *Mr. Angel*. In the film, people also look to your work as offering sexuality education. Do you position yourself that way? Have you thought about what kind of education we need around menopause?

BUCK: Yes. I am a big advocate for sexual health and expression, but it is not the only thing I want people to take from my work. I am also an advocate for self-love and just becoming yourself. I always think about how we could discuss menopause more within the trans community as well as the cisgender male community. I think menopause has in the past just been something people think is about being female, but it is clearly not only that. I think by starting this conversation it will make more people feel comfortable talking about it and remove some of the stigma that surrounds it.

E. D.: How do you feel about menopause career-wise? Is this wrapped up in aging generally? Or is menopause also explicitly about sexuality, about feeling sexual too? As we received submissions for the anthology, we noticed that some stories imagine an end to their sex lives, while others imagine a brand new beginning. I mean, really hot! Where do you see yourself on this spectrum?

BUCK: Career-wise I think it could be a great thing for me to start publically discussing. I don't see anyone within my community discussing it. Yes, for sure people mostly only see this as an aging thing. But it is not, it is also about hormone change and in the trans community that could mean so much more, because many younger people are going through the change at an earlier age and also having hysterectomies. Talking about this could help people deal with the mental and physical changes that happen during menopause.

I also think it is about sexuality because hormones are about sexuality. It is interesting how some people think menopause is the end to your sex life, whereas I think in many cases it's the beginning of a whole new body and a new way of feeling sexual. My life changed sexually with the use of hormones. I've always want to share that because I believe a healthy sex life is so important, especially for women going through this change. Is it because we have been told that your sex life is over during this time?

E. D.: That's a great question. Maybe this is why so many of our anthology submissions were about sex. You'd think more people would want to talk about not being able to have babies anymore. Instead it was like this cry-out: Don't write me off. I'm still a sexual human being. As Taryn Thomson says: "I plan to fuck my way right through my geriatric years." I love that line. The idea of being as sexy as you want as long as you're alive. Because after menopause, we still probably have a lot of our lives left to live. This is truer than ever before in history — and even more so for young people in the trans world. Do you think perceptions about growing old are part of the challenge?

BUCK: Growing old is always on everyone's mind, I think. Many people think that life is over when you hit fifty years. I was guilty of that, but I can tell you my life is better than ever and that includes my sex life. So again if we can start the dialogue and the younger generation sees the positive response around menopause and that it is not a sex death sentence, I believe this will change the way we think about it.

E. D.: I envy how comfortable you seem in your body. Sometimes during perimenopause, and often during menstruation, I've felt at war with my body. How has your comfort with your body evolved over time?

BUCK: I have been there with my body as well. It took years of re-training myself to feel the way I do today. I hated my body not only sexually but just in everyday life. I hated looking at myself, or even thinking about myself sexually, though I had a high sex drive. Being in my body at that time was torture for me, with lots of self-hate. It wasn't until I started to see the masculine changes in my body that I felt comfortable even looking at myself or felt comfortable enough to have others look at my naked body. This was a huge challenge and honestly I would never have thought in a million years that I would be the person who gets asked this question all the time. It's quite amazing and something I hope others can see is a possible place to be.

Flash Flood

COLETTE MAITLAND

In a flash,
droplets festoon
the hairline,
creeks appear
in those nooks
behind the ears,
feeding the shallow
pond between
the collar bones

And that space,
right there, between
the breasts, where moist
heat escapes like steam
from a bag of popcorn —
crevice, crevasse, cleavage?
Never mind.

Kneecaps *can* sweat,
so do the tops of feet —
all while he snores
next to me, quilt yanked
up to his chin!

My doctor says it
could go on for years

Jesus, I wish I were a man.

A woman at mid-life

SHIRLEY A. SERVISS

A woman at mid-life doesn't want
to be a wife. She needs her own
bed so she can roam to any side
she likes after night sweats drench
her sheets. She needs to turn on
the light at will to read or write if
flights of mind won't let her rest.

A woman at mid-life needs a
lover she can invite over
on days she wants to play
at pleasure. She doesn't want
him to stay and expect dinner.
She has other ways to spend
her leisure time.

The Hot Women

RHONA MCADAM

We are the hot women,
fused and dangerous,
steaming through sleep.
Vapours rise where we touch.

Hands on the coverlet
search the night
for youth's cool dream.

We unattended candles
lie radiant as glowing ash.

Water does not slow
this burn, it goes on and on,
subterranean as temper.

Sleep spills from our beds. We rise
in burning armies, hauled
from the molten deep,
to creak the halls, brittle
and precarious
on feet of fire.

TWO: IN/FERTILE

Life After Life

ARLENE S. BICE

Three days after having a hysterectomy, I was home from St. Francis Hospital and moving pretty slowly, inching my way across the kitchen and into a chair. I had made a light lunch and cleaned up and now looked forward to relaxing while I read a book. A neighbour knocked on my door. My son Guy had been in a boating accident. He had gone down into the river and had not come up. With that said and nothing more, the neighbour turned away and left me alone.

Dressing as fast as possible, trying to be careful of my stitches, I prayed, "Please, God, no. Don't let this be happening, let it be a mistake." My heart pounded to the rhythm of the words.

I wanted to run as fast as my mind was running, but couldn't. I took tiny steps, trying not to pull my stitches loose. Bordentown Beach was two blocks away but it might as well have been miles. The stitches pulled if my steps were too fast or too long. I was terrified that I would lose Guy and terrified that I would lose the work done by the surgeons.

At the end of the sidewalk, I inched my way forward to where the potholed gravel road splayed out to form a beach. Another obstacle. I forced myself to stay calm, at least on the outside, and took in the scene before me. Bordentown Beach is supposed to be a place for fun. It isn't sandy, but it's still busy. People usually gather on it to watch pleasure boats slide in and out of the river. Today they were standing in pairs and small groups, looking out at the water. I found a place to stand away from everyone. I didn't want to talk.

In my peripheral vision I could see heads turn toward me. I heard the whispers: "That's his mother." I moved closer to the water and watched the Hope Hose Humane First Aid Squad without understanding what they were doing. I couldn't ask them questions. I was too afraid my voice would break or I would cry. Instead, I eavesdropped. I overheard the word *dredgers* and knew a little more.

I had visions of Guy as the smiling baby he was, with his white blond hair and dimpled cheeks, of photos of him as a grinning kid in elementary school. I saw him marching around the house with his brothers in step with the children's music on the console. I recalled Christmas with Guy in his red-and-white Santa Claus outfit. I saw him in the Superman Hallowe'en costume I made for him. When he put it on, he leaped off the six-foot high back porch because he thought he would be able to fly. He was lucky that he didn't break a leg.

Someone had called my son Bret. My other son, Ralph, didn't live in town anymore. Bret now strode toward me from his truck. He was twenty-six years old, two years older than Guy. He kept his face rigid, but his emotions showed in his shoulders, his walk, and in his fists, balled up like he wanted to hit someone. Trying to keep the terror out of my voice, my words broke up as they jerked out of my mouth. If I began sobbing like I wanted to, the surgeon's handiwork would tear apart like my heart.

"He'll be okay. They'll find him." I said. "This can't happen twice in one family." I was referring to my other son Kenny who had passed away in a car accident six years earlier. He was twenty-four at the time. I never did get the whole picture of what happened on that dark, rainy night outside Washington D.C. It made his loss hard to accept.

Grief had created a dead zone inside me. I knew Kenny was gone but I had never gotten used to it. Sometimes I thought I saw him in a crowd then stopped short. I would remind myself, "Oh, no. He's gone." I could not believe that I could lose another son.

On this sunny afternoon, there were plenty of witnesses. People stood around discussing the accident. They would not approach me but they talked to Bret. He went over to a few of the fellows he knew.

When he returned to me, he filled me in on the details.

"Guy was staying in to watch the game on TV. He'd been out late the night before and didn't want to go anywhere. But Bud wanted to put his new boat in the water and needed Guy's help."

Guy was always conscious of a friend's need. And of the two, he was the ace swimmer. How ironic. Damned ironic. The boat tipped and flipped. Bud managed to get to the shore. Guy didn't. When he couldn't see Guy in the water, Bud ran for help.

Bret jammed his hands into his jeans pockets and wandered off into the nearby woods. Minutes later, I heard his scream, an animal sound, like the screech of a banshee. People started to run toward the woods, but I held up my hand to stop them.

I knew what was happening. Bret was in agony. He needed the trees around him, not people asking him questions. I still recall the chilling sound Bret made that day, the sound of despair. It's buried deep inside me.

I clung to the idea that Guy had swum to the Pennsylvania side of the river. He was an excellent swimmer and had learned to swim underwater with his eyes open before he could even walk. When the boys were little, their father, a mason contractor, had built a cinder block swimming pool in the yard for them. It was about two and a half to three feet high. The summer before Guy turned a year old, he swam as naturally as a fish. He was fearless. And he was a union stonemason, strong in the arms and upper body. It didn't make any sense to me that he could drown in the river.

The day slipped by with no signs of Guy. My stitches pulled from standing so long; my strength drained. My mind raced with more images of Guy. I remembered how the birthing pains I had with Guy were all in my lower back. It had felt as though my spine was cracking into two pieces. A gurgling baby came from that pain. What could possibly come from this?

People drifted off, tired of waiting. Others arrived, curious. Some of Guy's friends heard about the accident and, hoping it was not true, they came to join the vigil. Guy had a lot of friends. He was a congenial sort.

Afternoon turned into evening and I walked the two blocks home to get a sweater. The early June air was turning cool. Any hope of finding Guy was fading. But I couldn't give up. I held onto the thought of his excellent swimming.

Mayor Gloria Schooley joined me when I got back to the beach. She stood by my side, sometimes making small talk, as people do. Sometimes she just stood there in silent comfort. She was the first female mayor of Bordentown City, and I knew she was not there as an official but as a mother and as someone who cared. She stayed by my side until the wee hours of the morning when it was time for me to go home. I felt drained, like my reproductive system they'd removed only three days before was going to fall out again.

When I returned to the beach the next morning, the crowd was gone and the dredgers had pulled their gear out of the river. I took my leaden self home and waited as millions of mothers have waited. I was a zombie. My insides were dead.

"What the river takes," they said, "it will give up in three days." Three days later on June 9, Guy's body was found snagged along the river's edge in Fieldsboro, the next small hamlet south of Bordentown. His body was recovered and taken to Huber's Funeral Home. I cried then. This was the third time I had needed to call Huber's in six years. My son Kenny passed away in '82, my mother in '86, and now in '88 I had lost Guy. Grief was no stranger to me. I cried with my two remaining sons and in the arms of Guy's many friends who had come to say goodbye. I cried into my pillow. I cried all the tears I had held back before.

It was Bret who identified the body. He saved me the agony of seeing what a river does to someone after three days. Because of Bret, I could remember Guy alive and happy.

In the year after his death, Guy's spirit visited me from time to time. He would flick the lock of hair behind my right ear and I knew he was with me. One day when I was at the cash register at my bookshop, a lady came through the open door and walked toward me.

She smiled and said, "Oh, your son is standing behind you!" I must have gone pale. She said, "Oh! I'm so sorry. I hope I didn't upset you. That just popped out." She covered her open mouth with her hand as if to shove the words back in.

I smiled. I had already sensed he was with me.

It took me ten years before I could talk about Guy's death with Bret or Ralph. Ralph and Guy had been close, less than two years apart in birth and as tight in friendship as identical twins.

"I just don't understand it, what with Guy's swimming ability," I said to Ralph.

"The boat was a small one, more suited for just one person," Ralph said. "When it flipped up, it must have hit Guy on the forehead and knocked him out."

That made sense. Now I knew. He had not struggled facing death as he had struggled in his young life. Guy's time on earth was over and, in some realm, he was a truly happy kid again. His visits to me proved that. The awful emptiness I felt not understanding what had happened began to heal.

Giving birth, I never expected to outlive two of my four children. It is so unnatural. Yet I have. As a result of my losses, I have read about what happens when someone dies, about life after life. I find comfort knowing that, although I am without two of my sons, they have completed their journey for this lifetime and we *will* meet again. We will live another lifetime together. Hopefully a longer lifetime.

To love completely is to let someone go. Mothers who lose children suffer the pain of giving birth and the pain of grief. My hysterectomy was a part of that loss, too. Part of what made me a woman was gone.

I Am My Mare

LISA COUTURIER

When I first met Tyra, my Icelandic mare, she was in a dark, dusty stall. I made a kissing sound to get her attention, as one does with horses, but she refused to look my way. Or any other way. She was possibly the least likely horse to buy. Her palomino, golden-furred body was not tight, taut, and equine-athletic. Her belly, like mine, had a multiple-baby sagginess and her rump, like mine, showed evidence of yearly expansion. When I reached out to touch her, she trembled and her eyes darted to the stall door. All of this made it abundantly clear that that she'd probably rather buck me off than let me ride her, which, if it happened at all, would be a long-term negotiation.

Concerned that Tyra's behaviour would cause me not to take her, her owner explained, "Awwww, she's shy."

She may have started out shy at her first farm in Idaho, but somewhere on her way through West Virginia, or Maryland where I found her, it was obvious that she wasn't shy anymore. She was pissed off.

Aside from using Tyra as a broodmare, few people had spent time with her as an individual horse. As they age, broodmares become less useful as a means of making money, and many horse folk in my area have a tale about other horse people — the bad ones — leaving an older broodmare to rot in a field. Without attention or care over the years, broodmares are often unrideable and skittish. Tyra was entering that stage and now was a "for sale broodmare" which is kind of like being an old woman in a bar. She had endured years of being mounted by shaggy stallions, years of pregnancies, years of surrendering to men's arms snaking up her vagina to check on the progress of her unborn foals, years nursing foal after foal, years of being stuck in stalls. It was no wonder she was reluctant to acknowledge me. For all she knew, I was just the next human in a long line of humans willing to subject her body to procedures she preferred not to tolerate.

I have been told, mostly by horse people who make money from breeding, not to get too emotional — that is, too liberal and *menopausal* — about the horse business and the broodmares left behind. Horses, whether mares or geldings, are immeasurably more powerful than any human and can break most leather tethers with the strength of their necks. Still, horses do what is asked of them — even when they are asked cruelly. Then they wait and watch. They give people chance after chance to do the right thing, even if we rarely do it, even if we never do it, all of which reminds me of myself and my relationships with people. Standing there in her stall, Tyra was like the main character in *The Yellow Wallpaper*. She was a female forbidden from expressing herself and whose true desires were ignored. She was bored and confined and, quite possibly, slowly going insane. In other words, at the time, I was thinking Tyra and I just might be at a similar point in our lives, emotionally.

Which meant Tyra was the mare for me.

I already had three geldings at home. And my own daughters, little fillies themselves, were starting — dare I say it, because they never want me to say it — *menstruation*, just as I was beginning to leave it behind. Everything about my daughters was young and silky and fresh and popping and gorgeous and sassy. I needed a female around who was more like me. I needed a perimenopausal broodmare. I needed Tyra.

A few months after I bring Tyra home, I find an article that links the lives of mares and women, entitled *The Mare Model for Follicular Maturation and Reproductive Aging in the Woman*. The article explains that the physical factors causing menopause are more alike between women and mares than, say, between women and rodents, who have ten babies at a time. It would make sense, it seems to me, to compare women to cows who, like us, have one baby at a time, but unfortunately cows and calves become hamburger, steak, and veal before they reach their bovine menopause. Although that's not how the researcher explains it. She is more vague in her description, saying of the bovine fate, "Relatively few of these animals are maintained until old age." Mares are kept around for twenty or more years, so their natural reproductive lives can be tracked. Apparently Tyra and I have both maintained our dwindling number of oocytes for decades, and now our little eggs of fiery life are burning out. The sun of our fallopian tubes is setting. I am my mare; my mare is me.

Of course Tyra doesn't give a damn about any of this. She doesn't know what I know about menopause, or think what I think about menopause. Which doesn't mean she doesn't think. She just thinks different things. Through the winter, I notice how much Tyra enjoys the simple pleasure of being alone, especially when it's cold. One early morning after a night of sleet and high winds, it's obvious she's left the barn and my other horses behind for the delights of foul weather. I find her standing by herself in the centre of the outdoor riding arena. Her nearly foot-long, shocking white mane, whipped up and curled by the wind, stands as erect as Billy Idol's Mohawk along her neck, frozen in place and shining with ice crystals.

I walk toward her, the sky still spitting, the sun barely rising through the gray air of our land. She reaches for me with her wide, black velvet nose, sniffing and snorting, her breath rising in steam around her eyes. We stand together in the stillness and the dark and the cold, our primordial follicles perishing. The early morning crows blast by overhead.

The Things We Carry

TANYA COOVADIA

Last January, I attended a reading series during which two distinguished male authors, in separate opening remarks, said derogatory things about middle-aged women. I don't think I would have noticed twenty years ago, but lately, for some reason, I am particularly attuned to discussions regarding women of my uncertain age, especially when they are uttered in tones suggestive of a shameful affliction.

Benign anal tumours, say.

One of these men, after his reading, went on to add further insult. He described the typical bumbling misapprehension of his work by that admiring but clueless fan who, he assured us, in his laconic drawl, was "always a middle-aged woman." As a late-blooming member of the midlife sisterhood, this incident sparked a poem in me.

And (in a laconic drawl) it's dedicated to Tim O'Brien.

Always a Middle-Aged Woman
(because middle-aged men are just men)

Striding up
with her staunchly held head
her opinions bared like wrinkled breasts

And those years she wears

a bitter glory of furrows and lines
etched by thousands of erstwhile smiles.

Who do they think they are,
these ladies (and we mean you, ma'am)
thriving so steadily
from their cloak of invisibility

We don't see your once young face
we never stroked your once shining hair

We can't hear your
sweet, barely caught breath
because you're
Blatantly!
middle-aged

As though aging is some kind of victory
as though youth and beauty
are not mandatory

As though you can bring
something new to the world
when your womb is too old to care.

My mirror,
I,
we,
you
reflect this, true

We lift our jowls toward our ears
and smile

a spasm, a rictus. Of youth.

On Women and Forest Fires

C. E. O'ROURKE

All is not lost in
   this little death
as fire rages through the forest
   pine cones burst open
create new life
   after so long being ordinary
time to uncover the core
   unencumbered
by the hard shell of waiting

this alchemy
   requires intense heat
   wise women know
as the Pine knows
   the advantage of delayed bloom
is that it doesn't matter now
   what anyone thinks
   this is freedom
the fire of my flourishing
   will burst open in due time
the serotinous cone blooming
   like a flower

curling back onto itself
   releasing the resinous constraints
exploding embryonic ingenuity
       proliferous potential
       like perfect fireworks
on warm soil
       worth the wait

Up at Two in the Morning

CAROLINE BOCK

You wake me in the middle of the night again: burning up, slick to the touch, smelling of sweat and traces of lavender, once your primary scent. I don't know how you can sleep. You roar, snoring, breathe out of your mouth. You scuffle with yourself in your old white bathrobe, and it flies open and your breasts, oh my God, I want to reach out and hold them up for you. I have buried myself in those breasts. I have even tasted milk from those breasts just to see what it was like — and it was watery, and laced with garlic you said was from the pizza we had shared. You also claimed that our son didn't care if you tasted of garlic. I wasn't sure whether to believe you, even though you said it like so many things, with absolute confidence. But if I touch you now and wake you — I won't. You say you never sleep through the night anymore. Still, it's me who always seems to be staring into the dark, debating whether I should go into the guest room and see if I can fall asleep on that lumpy bed, between those scratchy new sheets. I hate to sleep alone, but I have to sleep too. If I nudge you, you might turn over at least. But before I can manoeuver my arm, you mumble in your sleep. I hold my breath, listen. I want your words to be some insight into you, or us. Sometimes I don't understand how I got here in this king-size bed next to you. But it's your sister's name and you're yelling at her to get out. Get out. We've been married how many years? Thirty this June. And in your sleep you are still fourteen or fifteen fighting with your kid sister. I sigh and tuck my cold hands between my legs, feeling out of time, neither young nor old, as if I will exist only for this moment and then disappear. I will leave. Get something to drink. Water. Check the score on the game. Check e-mail. Soon enough, you fall quiet. Your hair, damp and curled, wilds onto my pillow. You ask me all the time if I see any grey and I swear every time I see none. I will never admit that you've gained weight either. All I know is that your nipples are the size of berries, as large as mulberries, and the moon is streaking through the window and I can't help myself. With the tip of my tongue, I taste them and they are salty and warm and familiar and good, and I know I will be here when you wake.

The Brothers Germain

E. D. MORIN

At half past five, Sam sets the glue brush down on her worktable and inspects the tiny vacuum cleaner. She rotates the piece with care, tilting her head, clucking quizzically, asking herself if this bone sculpture is still relevant. With all the noise out there, she's not so sure. She smoothes her paint smock absently, her fingers restless, and there's the sting — her left thigh tender from the needle and ink punctures. Twin swallows chasing each other's tails. She recalls the hours reclined in the tattoo artist's chair, this tolerance for pain she didn't know she had. Her hand moves across her thigh and she smiles, closes her eyes.

The tattoo reminds her that relevance is irrelevant. She has always hated rules. She has always hated convention. She is her mother's daughter, in love with two men more than fifteen years her junior. The beautiful brothers Germain.

Piper and Tyrrell bash through the door, home from the gallery. Their entrance is boisterous. Mid-story, in the middle of a stupid gag, they stomp through the house in their boots, fists laden with plastic bags. Bursting with male bravado, they parade past her studio to the kitchen where they crack open dark brews and begin their Monday ritual. Wing night.

She always ends up joining them, not for the glistening red wings (she doesn't eat meat) but for their infectious youthful hijinks. Every Monday night they perform for her. There's an unwritten rule they will leave gallery politics behind. There's another unwritten rule that says any rule is verboten.

When Sam enters the kitchen, Tyrrell is telling a story about the new female intern they have taken on in the gallery framing shop.

"So she's asking me what jig to use."

Piper adds chili peppers and maple syrup to the sauce bowl. "Go on."

"I tell her, you're the boss. You pick. And of course it's the wrong jig."

"Of course."

Of course? Jesus.

Tyrrell strips the cellophane off a boat-sized package of chicken wings. "It's entirely the wrong weapon."

"You let her ruin the frame." Piper starts in. "Tell me you didn't—"

"Nah uh. Better than that."

Sam can already tell where the story is going. The unsuspecting intern is the target of one of their pranks and, as usual, Tyrrell's account is peppered with lewd military jargon. She feels sorry for the unwitting young woman, but Sam keeps quiet and maintains the Monday code. No gallery politics. Enjoy the show. If there are any real transgressions, she can bring them up later. She has her ways.

Tyrrell moves to the sink and begins rinsing the meat. He places the wings on a clean tea towel and pats them dry. The raw chicken flesh is revolting. But these wings feed her sculptures, after all. Her tiny bone machines. She recalls that Tuesday morning, over a year ago, when she found the detritus of another wing night in her best ceramic bowl, and had on impulse dumped the mess into a pot, boiled, dismantled, cleaned, and dried the wings, and from their skeletal parts had built her first bone sculpture. A tiny domestic robot. Who knew what that act would lead to?

Tyrrell arrives at the end of his story. "Rat a tat tat, dusted," he says, punching the air with imaginary gunfire.

"You better believe it," Piper adds wryly, ever the elder brother, even if it's by less than a year.

At the gallery, Piper runs the show. Under his direction, Tyrrell cuts glass and matte board, builds frames for art pieces, and mounts them on the walls. For Sam's recent show, *The Bone Machine*, Tyrrell erected curved stud walls and built all the platforms. He drywalled and rolled on coats of white gallery paint. Then, under Piper's precise curation, he positioned and repositioned her sculptures on the platforms until the elder Germain was satisfied.

Piper can be a control freak in the gallery, but together they make a good trio. Sam creates, Piper curates, and Tyrrell completes. The atmosphere is civil. These brothers know how to be good feminists.

But on wing night, something else happens. She's at a loss. She can't explain it.

The throttle of engines breaks Sam's sleep. Outside, husky female voices shout over the engine rumble. Sam props herself up, jaw stiff and gritty, and squints over Tyrrell's unshaven chin to the clock's glowing digits. One-eleven. She groans and collapses onto her pillow. The bed is a king, wide enough that she can nestle between them without touching either, unless one exceeds his allotted space. Tonight, she can't sleep for their heat. Sweaty and annoyed, she wants to extricate herself from the covers, kick out from between them, and holler at these neighbour biker chicks, launch a salvo of obscenities. Open fire. *Get your derrières in gear and move the fuck along!* Just like her mother.

Instead she slides her palm across the mattress and touches Tyrrell's midriff. He is her grounding rod. He could sleep through an earthquake, she is certain, or the end of the world. He is so utterly transparent. As for Piper, how to tell what is in his head?

These noisy engines could leave her spinning for hours. She massages her jaw and surrenders to these biker chicks, picturing them: not the shampoo commercial types — no perfect tresses coiled under helmets and released with a sexy flourish — but sporting barber cuts. Leather-clad legs straddling huge Harleys, owning the street, defiant. She might have aspired to their female bravado once.

But it is one-eleven in the morning.

Three bones, she can hear Tyrrell say. He loves abusing the word bone, loves its layered meanings, especially since *The Bone Machine*. Last night, at eleven minutes past eleven, it was four bones, a continuation of the wing night spectacle. Sam presses her knuckle to her cheek. Outside, the noisy throttle sets her off again. *Move the fuck along!*

This is not the first time she's noticed her mother in her. Last week in the garden, she gave refuge to an injured songbird. Her mother would have done that too. So hopelessly naive. The songbird's breast was throbbing madly, one wing broken and an eye socket pecked out. Sam knew it was pointless, she knew she was interfering with nature, but she couldn't stand to leave it there and simply return to her worktable as though this little drama were not unfolding right in front of her. So she brought the bird inside and set it in a small turquoise bowl on the windowsill. A finch, she was almost certain. She might have dug up worms for it to eat, or found an eyedropper to dispense water, but she resisted, knowing the futility of the act. She was the interloper. She was meddling in avian affairs. Better to leave the poor finch on the windowsill with a view of the mountain ash and its bright red berries.

Her mother would have stayed to witness its dying breath. Probably, she would have cried. Sam simply became engrossed in her work. Such is the amnesia she is capable of, this ability to blot out news, bad or good, anything beyond the confines of her studio. And then, with her ward long forgotten, Piper came into the studio holding the turquoise bowl. His face was pale.

"You found my finch."

"It's disgusting." He glared at the bowl. "And dead."

Rosie. That was the name her mother gave every bird, as if each were her pet, her confidante even. As if the avian *umwelt* was in any way knowable.

Other people were as unknowable as finches, each isolated inside their human *umwelt* or bubble, destined to be distinctly apart. Piper *was* shaken, and how to explain that? She couldn't. The brothers served up a mound of dead bird flesh every Monday night. What was this, then? A transference of grief?

The engine rumble continues. The women break hoarsely into a chorus, shouting over their motorbikes, drunk or stoned or high on something. Still in their twenties, Sam guesses, their singing blatantly deep-toned and boyish. It's a wonder one of her neighbours hasn't come out.

Tyrrell is softly snoring. She wonders if Piper is awake.

Sam thinks of Piper and his magic sleep aid. He grinds his teeth too. She still bristles when she recalls her visit to Piper's dentist, the infantile blue whales on the dental clinic walls. After years of grinding her teeth, she was willing to try whatever the dentist proposed. A moulded thermoplastic appliance for her lower teeth, he suggested, just like Piper's. But as Dr. Maligne was about to take an imprint, he called the thing her binkie. Seriously?

Sam feels her skin grow hot. She wonders if this is a female thing. She wonders if this is the treatment the dentist gives to women and kids. She had held it up and asked Piper. "What does Dr. Maligne call this thing?"

"A dental guard. Maybe an appliance. Why?"

She didn't bother explaining. "What do you talk about at your appointments?"

"We talk about art."

"You're kidding me." Sam fumed.

Sometimes, in the quiet of her studio, she is so infuriated with men, she wants to launch her bone sculptures at them like Tyrrell's missiles. Her sculptures are selling, they have hit a cultural nerve of sorts, but sometimes she wishes her art had real power. She's afraid she's wasting her time.

She can tell Piper is awake now. She moves to him, her hair falling in a silver glow. She is fully awake. Her mother's voice in her ear whispers, "This is what crazy is."

Piper's hands move to the soft curve above her hips. He skates his fingers down her left leg, presses against her tattooed swallows.

Sam winces, moves Piper's hand. "There," she whispers.

Piper removes his night guard, sets it atop Wharton's *Icefields*, part of his research for the gallery's next show.

Sam wrestles Piper and straddles him, pinning him to the pillow. He makes a show of wiggling out from under her, then easily surrenders. "You win."

"Shhh," she whispers, glancing over at Tyrrell. He is still out cold.

The engine resonance enters her. Tyrrell would say he'd hit her sweet spot; he'd call himself the missile. Tyrrell is so beautiful, but why this military jargon? Where does he get it? Guns and ammunition, the training of arms, on her, his ground zero. *Let's flip to see who'll be tail gunner*, he'll say to Piper.

She is hot. She has spent her currency with Piper, burned up the night with her fury. Meanwhile, these crazy biker chicks continue to race their engines — as if oil were a limitless resource, as if this were broad daylight. She should open the curtains and bang on the glass, show them what crazy is. She rests on her back between Piper and Tyrrell, not touching either one.

This looming threshold. She is her mother's only child. She has never wanted to be a mother. Her sculptures are babies enough. Yet what must it be like to be a mother? The threshold is disappearing, falling behind her. When her mother birthed her, it was at home with a midwife, no instruments, no painkillers. Is the pain of birth anything like a tattoo?

Piper whispers in her ear. "They're saying things about us."

Another one of his gags, she supposes. "They're not. They can't hear us over their engines."

"Not the bikers. Your fans. They're saying things about the three of us."

She feels penned between them, these brothers. She wishes she could carve a wider space in the mattress. Her fans? This talk is the reason she hates her métier sometimes, the need for buyers, the need for a gallery, these art connoisseurs who think they can purchase her. Moneybags who jest that she too would go nicely inside their Spanish villas.

"They want to know what we do in bed. And which brother is your favourite."

Her skin feels sticky.

"And which of us is the alpha male," Piper adds.

"Seriously? Why do people even care about these things?" Sam swallows a grin, knowing which of them is alpha. She is.

She slides out between the brothers and off the end of the bed. Sleep is impossible. She will fill the kettle, boil water for tea, make her sleepless night official. She will begin another sculpture, another household machine, another space-age artefact from the domestic prison. In a radiant brainwave Sam sees a birthing apparatus. Robot-operated forceps.

At the bedroom window, she yanks open the curtains and raps noisily on the glass. She squints. Through the headlamp glare she sees these aren't women bikers after all. They are bearded. The men stare, their grins goofy and lopsided. Sam wavers. She is naked. Wilderness on one side, caged animal on the other. But which side is which?

Barely tolerating their gaze, Sam glares back. She flips them the bird.

"Dusted," Tyrrell croons.

Something has finally woken him. Sam turns to say something but Tyrrell is already vaulting off the mattress, throwing his arms around her, hugging her.

She shuts the curtain. "None of your business," she whispers at the glass.

Tyrrell takes her by the hand and pulls her back to bed.

Unconventional Wisdom

MERLE AMODEO

Despite all the evidence against it,
I thought I'd be wise
when I reached sixty.
The truth, I've discovered,
is we don't grow wise,
we grow careful.

We stop taking chances,
learn to hedge our words,
and not commit.
Then we grin like the Cheshire cat,
and shake our heads at the young, the brave, the naive.

But now and then a spark flares
to show our souls
haven't turned to ashes.
I dreamt last night that I asked
a handsome stranger to come home
and stay in my bed
until we'd done
everything I'd missed
for the last ten years.

When he was completely exhausted,
I forced him to give me
his brother's address.
It must have been a dream
but I'm not giving up the address
scrawled on my sheet
till I've checked it out.

Her Love Life

GEMMA MEHARCHAND

She didn't have a death wish
Didn't want to kiss strangers
Just because they came to the same party
Did not sniff glue or gasoline
Did not drink or smoke
So when she found herself in love with one person
After another she felt intrigued by her hormones
And slipped away from sainthood
Into the dark night of sex
Which proved to be friendly
But eventually she gave it all up
Lived quietly ever after
As she had when she was fifteen.

Roll Over a Change Is Coming

MAROULA BLADES

I can cook, but not for the next forty years.
I want to see mammoth thighbones
on plates instead of chicken giblets,
so I can conk him. K.O.
Xena style.

I can iron, but holes will appear in his sleeves
if he doesn't lift hot metal to brand his arse with:
I can do it; it doesn't take balls.
I love to hoover, but at times,
I wish the damn thing were bigger,
big enough to fit a beer belly and scrambled eggs.

I love to make love,
but I'm not the missionary visionary anymore.
I want to lie on red satin sheets with silver,
thin chains woven through the shine,
and I want loads and loads of French black,
lacy bras with holes at the peaks,
so my nipples can see what I'm doing for a change.

Roll over Meathead, I'm coming.
Here's your Indian take-away, hot and spicy,
hot to sizzle the beer in your guts,

get on down with the onion rings, get your freak on.
Make some noise, *Ooh ah*.

I'm out of here on a five-day rail trip,
dressed combat style; inside I'm slinky,
a sack full of stringy lace is slung
over my love rocking hips.
I can feel the bumps from Wonder
poking out like ostrich eggs, ooh,
it feels good to sit on the climax of things.

The next best thing to "fxxx you"
are ham sandwiches and slices of hard, hard currant cake
where you can find the occasional cherry. Pop.

Autumn Fields

MARGARET MACPHERSON

The station wagon is packed to the roof, the hatch barely closing. My husband Tom has cleaned the garage, something I've been after him to do for weeks, and now damaged sheets of drywall, a tricycle with two wheels, bits of scrap plastic, a cracked garden hose, an old bureau with no drawers, and my pram, my corduroy covered, hooded, huge, old-fashioned, sagging workhorse of a perambulator, are on their way to landfill.

"Want to come to the dump?" He rubs his gloved hands together in anticipation.

"You've got the pram."

"Oh, that." He steps toward me, torn between comforting and cajoling. "It's done its time, Paula. It's served us well. You know yourself, the springs are shot on one side."

I feel like he's talking about me. Springs shot. I haven't had a period in eight months and the real thing that is shot is my temper. I'm either crying or I'm angry beyond reason. And now he's tossing away something precious.

All of my babies have ridden in that buggy. All of them have slept in it, out in the backyard at the foot of the stoop, with nothing but the canopy of our broad-leafed elm between their sweet eggshell cheeks and the sloping afternoon sun. Natalie and Jen, the twins, used to stand on the rails and hang on while I'd wheel Will down the road. They loved riding shotgun like that, leaning forward into the hood of the thing like joint figureheads

89

on a massive land yacht. It was my method of transportation for years. Before we splurged and bought our second car, all four of us would plow through the autumn leaves or the sludge of spring, the pram at the heart of our passage.

"But, I thought we might fix it." My feeble protest is lost in the scrape and shuffle of the garage door swinging down to block my view of newly ordered garden tools and our six bicycles suspended from the ceiling by their steering posts. Even Will rides a two-wheeler now. Has done for, what, six years? How did they grow so fast? Where did the time go?

"We?" He smiles and slaps his leather-gloved hands together again, anxious to get underway. "We're done with all this baby stuff and thank God. It couldn't be soon enough for me. Come on, the dump closes early on holidays."

It's Thanksgiving Day, a day of rot and ruin, but at least the snow hasn't come yet and the wooden Adirondack chairs seem to hunker down on the grass, obstinate and reluctant to be stored. The sunlight on their broad arms and deep, low-slung seats makes their primary colours glow, and with my sunflowers only slightly wilted and the hearty heads of marigolds still poking through the limp foliage of frost nipped tomato plants, I can almost imagine August.

"Paula. Paula? Hey, you coming or not?"

"What about the kids?"

"Allison will mind them. I'll tell her we're going."

He swings back into the yard and tramps to the back door, hollering at our eldest daughter, who is half-heartedly practicing the piano. As soon as he moves through the door, the tortured music stops. They are consulting and both appear on the back landing.

Allison is thirteen and a half, a tall, slender child totally unaware of her own pony-tailed loveliness. She was my serious baby, shy even, and cautious about each new discovery. She was born late in our relationship and I was a cautious new mother despite having the experience of a career. Shades of that early reticence still lingers in her personality.

"How long will you be gone?"

"Forty-five minutes, an hour, tops."

"Just keep an ear open and half an eye on them, Allie," I say. "Cut up an apple for Will if he's hungry. Natalie and Jen are playing ponies so they probably won't even know we're gone."

"I don't feel great."

Tom ignores her. "Oh, come on, Al. You can give the piano a rest and get some fresh air. You guys have time for the park if you leave right away."

"The park's for babies. We'll hang here." She smiles reluctantly at her daddy.

"Thanks, kiddo," he says, ruffling her hair. "Maybe we'll even bring you back a treat from the dump." He's down the stairs in a second and doesn't see her roll her eyes.

"What's wrong?" I ask. It's the fretting mother voice, not the rough-and-tumble cheer of her daddy. It's the only voice I've got left these days. My mother voice has consumed all the others.

"Oh, nothing." The screen door bangs and she's gone. A trill from bass to treble is her flippant farewell to practicing. In my mind's eye I watch this rush past the piano and see her flop onto the couch, reaching for her latest book. She's taken to reading my novels — Laurence, Atwood, Drabble — because *they last longer*. I shake my head and climb into the car.

"It smells funny in here."

"Roll down your window. We've got a date at the dump."

Tom's in a good mood. He likes order and he's achieved some semblance of that in the garage. The smell proves it. So I roll down my window and settle back in the passenger seat. It's a glorious autumn afternoon and getting out of the city lifts my spirits.

"Did you used to bring things back from the dump?" I ask.

"Oh, yeah. My dad was a great picker. I think it was the handyman in him. He'd bring stuff home that someone had tossed because they didn't know how to fix it. Mostly electric gizmos, small fiddly stuff he'd tinker with in the basement." Tom laughs. "I remember one winter he spent hours rebuilding this appliance that had an electric can opener on one side and an ice crusher on the other. Replaced the motor and everything. He must have got his wires crossed somewhere because when my mom went to open a can of soup the whole machine started shaking like crazy.

Tomato soup sprayed all over the kitchen. She threw the darn thing out in the yard, she was so mad. An ice crusher, imagine. Just what we needed in January."

I do imagine it. I see Tom and his brothers laughing madly while the gadget dances across the kitchen counter splattering thick red blobs of condensed soup across the frosted windows. I see Tom's father's face, amazed at his agitating creation. And I see his mother on her knees afterward, dishcloth in hand, cleaning the mess off the cupboard fronts, the fridge, the floor. The dishwater is the colour of blood.

When she opens the back door and heaves the piece of dump junk out the door, I applaud. I imagine its ridiculous weight sinking into a snow bank, disappearing for good. I feel sorry for Tom's mother, a woman in a household of men.

My husband is a man in a household of women. His father used to bring things home from the dump. My husband takes things there. *My* things. *My* pram.

The afternoon I found out our fourth and final child would be a boy — the son we had barely dared to hope for — the twins were sleeping in the pram. All too familiar nausea had sent me to the doctor. He warned me I was too old. He told me to be satisfied with the three girls and I remember feeling slightly guilty looking at the twins slouched together in the belly of the buggy, all sweat and curls, plump little limbs entwined, exhausted from the fresh air and missed afternoon nap. They had just turned three and I had barely recovered from their toddler days. I was happy, all right, but it seemed a betrayal to the girls, as though they weren't enough.

I tried to hide my pleasure at a boy, wanted to surprise Tom, but he guessed right away by the way my secret knowledge played on my mouth.

When Will came, Allison claimed him as her own. The twins were an indisputable unit who allowed an older sister into their play only when it suited them. But Will was wide open and ready to be loved. Allison spent hours playing with him, lugging him around the house, talking to him, dressing him up in her old clothes or the tattered cast-offs from the twins to further disguise his gender.

I let her take him out in the pram and they'd wheel around the block for hours, playing a game called Runaway Baby. She'd get the buggy up to speed and then let go, running alongside making faces at Will until the liberated pushcart came to a wallowing halt on the grassy boulevard. In her own way, she was practicing being a mommy and Will was her ideal guinea pig.

Will loved speed. He embraced danger right from the start. Clad in a drooping diaper and wispy floral blouse, he would transform innocent toys into weapons and make combat noises with his pouty, kissable mouth. Block towers would crash to the ground, helicopters were shot from the sky, ships would sink and vehicles were rendered wheel-less by the force of their fiery crashes. Will was my war baby.

He was also the one I least wanted to grow up. After Allison taught him how to tie his own shoes, he'd never let me help. He'd push me aside and I'd wait, exasperated, while he concentrated on making those two loops, that complicated cross-under of the bow. It would be so much quicker if he let me do it for him.

"You're pissed off about the pram, aren't you, Paula?"

Ah, perceptive Tom. So subtle, so delicate, so modern-man sensitive.

"No."

"Yes, you are. I can tell. You've hardly said a word."

"I was thinking about your mom, about the ice crusher."

"Okay." He swallows my lie because he doesn't want a fight. Neither do I, but it's there, anyway. A simmering thing I can't articulate.

We're on the outskirts of the city now, near the oil refineries. On my side of the highway, farmland rolls in fields of yellow and brown. Those swaths that haven't been harvested have been stooked. In a distant field, there's only stubble on the ground and, just beyond, the next field has been ploughed in preparation for spring planting. The farmers are readying for winter, the long season of darkness and dormancy.

Turning toward Tom is like looking into a different picture. His face is framed by giant industrial oil and gas plants, a massive tangle of pipes and stacks connected by lines to huge domed holding tanks. The refineries cluster together, four or five separate complexes belching smoke and steam and flared gas into the winter-quickened air. There's no down time here. Men work around the clock, seven days a week, 52 weeks a year. Tom worked the line for years until he got his ticket and moved up to management. Now he makes sure his guys keep production up, keep feeding the relentless processing system, the hungry maw of the machines.

"What do you want for supper tonight?"

He looks at me, puzzled. "I don't care."

"Well, someone has to care."

I can't believe my battleground is so small and domestic, so impossibly mundane. Tom doesn't take the bait. He's probably sorry he asked me to come.

We have to drive onto a large scale, which weighs our car before we arrive at the booth. A man in a blue uniform slides open the little glass window.

"Got any batteries, hazardous household goods, corrosives, or tires in there?" he asks.

"Nope. Couple of bicycle tires."

"No problem. It's a ten-dollar minimum per ton. Pay on your way out."

He waves us through the gates and we roll toward a parking lot at the edge of a man-made gully. Tom backs in and we both get out of the car. Below are dumpsters with large mechanical arms attached. The arms crank up and fall every minute and a half, pulverizing the material cast into the dumpster. It's efficient waste management. It's impressive and both of us watch in silence as the heavy crushing arm smashes the items in the dumpster before a mechanical rake drags the garbage out of the way.

"Oh, my."

Tom hands me his gloves and pops the hatch. We grab the garbage and start to throw it over the bank into the jaws of the crusher. I fling an old clothes line and some drywall board covered with chalk drawings from the children. Tom takes the bigger bits, the broken bureau and a rusted lawn chair, and heaves them over the side.

The pram, lodged at the back of the station wagon, is awkwardly compressed and we have to grab it on each side and pull the handle down to get it out of the car. We both struggle to get a grip low down and heave together, one on each side. The force of our release opens it up. The burgundy hood flops open, the compressed carriage spreads and for a moment it is full again, a baby buggy spinning its wheels in mid-air. It hangs suspended, beautiful and terrible, until it thuds to the bottom of the dumpster moments before the heavy arm descends. Although I close my eyes and look away, I hear the scream of metal upon metal and the yielding crunch of the frame. My pram is raked away.

"That'll be ten bucks," says the gatekeeper after our empty vehicle is re-weighed. We proceed in silence through the gates.

"Are you okay?"

The empty fields and the setting sun are no consolation and I am barely able to converse as we roll home. Why would he understand? How can I expect it of him? He no more cares for the pram than I care for the refinery. The refinery is relentless. It never stops. It is swallowing up all the farmland. Unproductive. Over. It's all over.

The house is warm, lit from within, when we return. Tom parks the car in the garage with a swollen sense of accomplishment. I hurry in through the back door, anxious to get away from him, to see my children, still so young.

The twins rush up. "Mom, Mom. It's Allison. Allison needs you." There is excitement, almost panic, in their fluttering bird voices. "She's in the bathroom and she won't come out."

I feel the weight of the day lift off and my feet become light as adrenaline rushes though my body. I hurry through the kitchen to the darkened hallway. There is a thin crack of light under the door.

"Allison? Allison, honey? Are you okay? Let me in. It's Mommy."

I touch the knob, expecting the door to be locked, but it turns in my hand. "Allison?"

She is sitting on the toilet. Her panties between her knees are stained a rusty burgundy. She looks up at me. And I stare back at her wide, expectant face but, for the life of me, I cannot speak.

A sprinter with pluck and panache

RONA ALTROWS

A sprinter with pluck and panache
Placed first in the hundred-yard dash.
She cried, "Ain't that nifty—
And me pushing fifty—
Whoops, here comes another hot flash!"

sixty

MARIANNE JONES

The birds' conversation takes on a manic edge:
It's spring and they have much to do.
I am not young like them, can't push any more.
I don't desire to move any more mountains.
I want to lie down at the feet of the hills and rest,
allow the birds to build nests in my hair;
let the grass grow over me, form a carpet of my skin;
the clouds float overhead, unmolested,
the winds disturb the trees, unchallenged.

Perimenopause

ALISON STONE

The moon
          unbinds her cords

Rogue wave, my body
     crests and crashes

to the staccato rhythm
  of last chances

womb frantic
with final eggs

Mommy, hurry up!
the children cry

Their sea glass eyes
            Their arms of sand

the year it did not flood

GERRY WOLFRAM

despite the expectations
of three female generations
spring came early in the
year it did not flood

no sudden flow
or guilty stain
of red upon
the sheets

she waited
braced herself
against the body's
old familiar ambush

months passed — *nothing* —
time no longer hinged
on periods (or any
other punctuation)

feeling not relief
(as she'd anticipated)

but a low regret-
ful ache

years later in hotel rooms
she'd still waken —
check the bedsheets
for familiar blood

These Things Did Not Happen

SHELLEY A. LEEDAHL

Not a wink of sleep the night before, and now in this clinic with ancient *Chatelaine* and *Parenting* magazines littered about the waiting room, Flora fears she is regressing into metaphors. A trapdoor has opened. Her limbs are anchored by chains that could topple Douglas firs. When the nurse calls her, she may not be able to move. This morning she could not get out of bed. She had wanted to stay buried beneath the quilt and stare at the sea-coloured curtains. Forever. She counted to a hundred before she swung her feet to the floor.

She is going missing piece by piece, except for the ominous lump — nothing like a baby — growing in her belly. No one notices this simultaneous withering and expansion. Not Harp, nor her son, Barry, whom they only see on Sundays, and always with his goat-faced wife who never offers to clear the table or do dishes.

"Flora Rolheiser, the doctor will see you now." Flora rises. The waiting room smells of urine.

"It's exhaustion," he says. She begins to explain but he talks over her, scribbling unintelligible words on his prescription pad. "I want to see you again in two weeks."

She joins the queue at the pharmacy in the clinic's basement. The man in front of her sports holes in the back of his neck, as if he's been attacked with a fork. Flora's turn. The pharmacist slides a bottle into a small white bag and folds the top over, then draws two fingers across the length of the fold. She does it again and Flora feels the tender spots behind her earlobes, beneath her pulse, where she and her siblings would press to torment each other as children.

In bed with Harp, she thinks that everything has something to do with blood. Her own menstrual blood didn't make an appearance until the very last day of Grade 8. She recalls running the mile home with her report card, happy about progressing from junior high to high school, then feeling the low cramp and strange wetness in her panties. Four blocks to go. At home she locked the bathroom door and there it was: the rust-red evidence that meant life would never be the same again.

She was the last among her friends to get her period. In Miss Hoffman's Grade 5 class at Jubilee School — a round school with classrooms orbiting the gymnasium — periods and pierced ears were the dual barometers of a girl's popularity. It was difficult to determine which earned more respect. Some suffered the pinch of the stud gun at Darlene's Hair Haven; others opted for the slower and messier home route — an older sister always willing and waiting with ice cubes, a potato, and a sewing needle. Flora coveted her week in the spotlight following Remembrance Day, 1974. Then the next set of virgin ears was sacrificed and someone else became the centre of the grade school universe.

The students — a Fortrel clad *mélange* of Donnas, Lindas, Cheryls, and Cindys — memorized states and capitals, wrote rhyming poems, and surrendered hours to Nancy Drew mysteries while twisting their gold studs or shepherd hooks and dabbing red, swollen lobes with hydrogen peroxide-soaked cotton balls. Disinfectant was the perfume of their youth, followed within the next few years by inexpensive cologne that smelled like a strawberry dessert. After the requisite number of weeks had passed, the girls euphorically graduated into *real* earrings. Flora's first two real pairs: round lavender studs shaped like Smarties that she purchased for five dollars at Rexall Drugs, and her mother's dangly crimson rhinestones that jingled when she shook her head.

As for menstruation, the girls took Midol for cramps, were excused from gym, and wore bulky sanitary napkins like their mothers did. The pads were held in place by a stretchy white belt that looked — Flora thinks about it now — confusing. The pad was like a mattress for Barbie dolls. Later, an adhesive strip would make the belts obsolete. Daring girls soon advanced to tampons — another type of graduation — but Flora took her sweet time.

Yes, everything has something to do with blood. And now that she has mostly dried up, there is new pain. A series of hard karate chops to her spleen. She stays folded until it passes, a caricature of an aged woman. Harp, beside her, is on his back. His foot is warm against hers. Soon he will be snoring. Something else to keep her awake. She rests both hands, priest-like, over the swelling. She lifts Harp's soft, warm fingers and asks: "Can you feel it?"

He probes for three seconds. "No, Flora. Go to sleep."

Easy for him. When did she last sleep through the night? She can't recall, maybe during that time she was hooked on prescription sleeping pills. Little, blue, foul-tasting bullets. Oh, they knocked her out. Kept her purring right through the night-sweats that soaked her sheets and finally had Harp moving into the bed in the spare bedroom some nights. "Jesus, woman, you're an inferno!" Didn't she know it. But eventually she needed to take two pills, and then even two could no longer knock her out.

A bang against the window. She starts. Surely a bird. Or a bat? Earlier that evening, at dusk, she stood out front beneath the flamboyant elms while brown bats swooped toward her. Begun as a test of faith, this twilight ritual is now habit. The bats fascinate and terrify in equal parts, like standing at the edge of a hurricane, or losing control of a cantering horse. The boulevard reminds her of the inner city neighbourhood where she grew up in a large white-pillared home that didn't belong to the street or the era. The ground sunk in graves around its perimeter. She and her brother set golf balls at one end of their parents' sloping bedroom floor and watched them roll to the other side. And once, a sleepwalking girl with a face as pale as an envelope and waist-length yellow hair knocked on their door at three a.m. and fainted.

She *thinks* that's what happened. But memory is a shapeshifter. That one might be from a movie. Years later, when she was telling the sleepwalker story to amuse Barry, she wondered if the blonde teen was also the one who scalded another girl with boiling water. The one who led them through the funeral home window to see a withered baby, small as a pound of butter. Perhaps these things did not happen at all.

Harp snores. She gives his back a gentle push and the snoring subsides. The clock ticks in the front room.

Harp says she's losing it. He says it's "The Change." An archaic expression. Witchy. A week ago he found her in the garden, the moon a chalk-smudge between lilacs. "Only the Italians know what to do with pears," she said. He peeled her fingers one by one off the shovel she was driving into the hearts of her hostas.

Weeks pass and she journeys a province away. She's never gone off alone — not once. She stares out the bus window into the fields of dirt-blown snow and skidoo tracks.

Banff. She thinks the water here will taste like rust, then takes a drink and there it is: rust. She fears it will make her sick. *Sicker.* She has no idea what the pills are supposed to do, but they have had zero effect on whatever is growing inside her. Why didn't the doctor give her something for *that*? Below the curve of her belly she cannot see her shoes. Sit-ups, the doctor advises.

Harp will find her note. She has left the hotel phone number. He will call soon. She has walked down the avenue of restaurants and expensive shops, has seen a fist-sized jawbreaker in a candy store for sixteen dollars, and has stared at the looming white-coned mountains until her eyes burned. She has watched the winter river, still open in spots, writhing and surrealistic. She has made a wide berth around three full-grown elk relaxing in the snow. Like the indifferent young girls working in the shops, they had paid her no attention.

She is not hungry for food. She is hungry for something she can't articulate. Has her existence mattered at all, to anyone? She doesn't know. She stops in front of a restaurant; in the end, one must eat, even without appetite.

"Are you waiting for anyone?"

She swallows. A Japanese couple in Norwegian sweaters — she had seen them unloading snowboards from their Subaru earlier — look sympathetically at her. She thinks they might invite her to join them. If they do, she will politely thank them, but say no.

She addresses the waitress's forehead. "Cockroaches can hold their breath for forty minutes. Did you know that?" Oh, why did she say that?

After the meal she returns to her room on Banff Avenue and lies down, still wearing her boots. She undoes the single pair of pants she can still fit into. Lycra. Ingenious. She can keep up a modicum of fashion. She shimmies the pants down over her soft flesh, spreads her fingers and lets them roam across her spongy skin — pushing, defining, measuring. Her cells multiply beneath her fingers. A kind of magic, like the hypnotist's show she saw as a teen, her own sister turned into a robot. One hypnotized man had tripped while under, and she remembers the blood on the floor where his head hit, the terrible sound of bone meeting concrete.

Everything has something to do with blood.

Her sister had been her parents' favourite. Older, more confident. Louder. You knew when she was in a room. Flora was the mouse; consequently, there were things she never got as a girl, things she wanted badly. A marionette. A blue dress that would bell around her legs when she spun. Sea-monkeys. You could order them from comic books, sprinkle the colourful crystals into jars of water and watch them grow. She had a friend who had a collection of snow globes. She had a friend who had won a slab of chocolate as big as a tabletop.

Flora closes her eyes and sees colours. Swirling. Monkey shapes.

When she wakes, shivering, the clock on the nightstand says two a.m. Harp hasn't called. She has come this long way and walked too much, and if she doesn't turn up the heat she will catch a cold. *Jesus, woman.*

Streetlights illuminate the wall and the bottom half of the bed. She pulls the curtain back an inch. Young people loiter in the hotel parking lot, smoking and laughing. One boy crushes a beer can with his boot.

Flora steps from the window. She fiddles with the heating system until the fan pushes out a dusty smell and masks the noise outside. She has always been calmed by the sound of forced air. As a girl she ate her Alpha-Bits while sitting directly on the register, the hot air puffing the nightgown around her knees. Back then she often thought about being a woman. She thought about kissing boys in cars or during slow songs at school dances. She thought about being called *Sweetheart*, or *Baby*. Now she feels she may die without ever having been loved.

She feels for the here-and-now nightgown in the small suitcase. She slips off her clothes, and there it is: her tumour, grown bigger in the last few hours, she is certain. She sits on the edge of the bed and muses. Her very cells acting out. Growing like a brand new planet.

October

STEVE PASSEY

Dry October, warmer than it used to be, like every October the last few years. Half the leaves were still on the trees, and half of those leaves still had some green. Mary Ann was in the hallway off of the kitchen leading to the front door with her granddaughter Peyton, who was clutching her swimming gear. A quiet and dreamy child, Peyton liked to swim and draw and never complained about anything.

"Let's go, Grandmamma," she said while Mary Ann slipped into her shoes.

Grandmamma was what grandmothers had been called in Mary Ann's family, going back unbroken to sometime during the Depression. Before that, too many grandmothers died. War and privations and migrations and such — no three generations of women of the same surname might actually be related. Peyton, who took French in school, had briefly delighted in calling Mary Ann *Grand-mère* but that only lasted through the French class, which Peyton had failed. (Or *Needed Improvement* as they put it.) She liked school, but not class, like her own mother at the same age.

"Hey Mary Ann," Jimmy hollered.

He was on the couch in the living room, watching college football. Jimmy always hollered; his hearing was starting to go. "Can you get me a Slurpee on your way back from the Facility? I'm feeling parched."

107

He pronounced Facility slowly, with equal emphasis on all four syllables. Fah-sill-eh-tee.

Mary Ann nodded but didn't answer. She walked out with Peyton into the sun, into the pale blue October morning. Peyton was into her side of the car, buckled up and ready for the pool before Mary Ann could open her door.

Peyton, all blue-eyed, single-braided, and serious, pulled up her knees. "Grandmamma, does Jimmy have any good qualities?"

Mary Ann thought out loud. "A couple."

"What are they?"

"It's nice having a second income in the house."

Peyton waited a little before saying, "And —?"

Mary Ann thought of Jimmy on the couch with a coke propped up on his belly. She was tempted to say "He don't fart — much." Instead she said, "Here we are at the pool."

Peyton unbuckled before the car stopped. "You gonna visit momma at the Facility?" She pronounced it the same way Jimmy did.

"I am. I'll be back in an hour. Have fun."

"Grandmamma. You're sweating." Peyton ran up the stairs to the pool.

Mary Ann checked the rear-view mirror. Beads of sweat crowded around her hairline, dampness lay up against her bra straps. She closed her eyes and leaned back and held her breath for a second as if that might leave her cool. Eyes closed, she thought of Jimmy's other good qualities. Last night, Jimmy didn't say a word when she cast aside the covers and got up out of her own undignified sweat, took a bed sheet from the linen closet and lay on the couch with the ceiling fan on and a window open to the cool October night. When she came out of the shower, she saw that Jimmy had gathered all the sheets and put them in the washer. When her daughter Mary Jean made one more mistake to add to a long list of mistakes and went into Custodial Rehabilitation, Jimmy didn't blame her. He never said anything. When Peyton came to live with them, Jimmy never said anything either. He'd moved in less than ten months before Mary Jean's arrest. The courts had a process. They had a system. The children's services people wanted interviews.

Again and again there was that phrase, Custodial Rehabilitation. A euphemism for a euphemism, like Facility.

Mary Ann told him, "No damn way any flesh and blood of mine is going into a foster home. If you don't like it, you can leave." Jimmy nodded. "I like it just fine, Mary Ann. I got your back."

That was all he said even as she raged against the world and the system and her stupid, stupid daughter and couldn't fall asleep. When she did sleep, she dreamt of winter and crows and trees so covered in cobwebs they were like statues in shrouds, and then the trees cracked under the weight of the webs and woke her up.

Jimmy's best good quality was this: he never referred to where Mary Jean was as prison. He always said *fah-sill-eh-tee,* and now that's how Peyton said it too.

Mary Ann was still too hot. Under the hooded sweatshirt, she wiggled out of her bra and stuffed it in her bag before putting the car in gear. She drove toward the Facility.

On her way, she always stopped at the convenience store and picked up chocolate bars and magazines for Mary Jean. She had to rush. It took longer than it should to get in to visit Mary Jean, and she only had so much time while Peyton was swimming. It usually meant a half hour visit and the risk of a speeding ticket. Sweating still, she parked and hustled into the store without locking the car doors. She gathered up as many two-for-one chocolate bars as she could carry in two hands. She glanced at the Slurpee machine longingly. Ever since Jimmy brought it up she'd craved one, but she was too short for time now. At the cashier, she set the chocolate bars down, picked up some Hollywood scandal rags and a *Women's Holistic Health* and laid them on the counter. She absent-mindedly read the *Women's Holistic Health* cover and noted one headline, in acid yellow letters:

The Average Woman gains 10 pounds during menopause
AND IT NEVER COMES OFF!
WILL THIS BE YOU?

"Goddamn!"
The clerk stared back silently. "Nothing," she said before the

clerk could ask. She paid and stuffed the *Women's Holistic Health* in the garbage bin on her way out.

She drove on an avenue lined with trees. The gold leaves fell slowly, one at a time, in the wake of her passage. Maybe it's not me, she thought. Maybe it's global warming. Phytoestrogens. Things she heard on television, or read in magazines. Things that made everybody sick. She drove five kilometres above the speed limit with the A/C blowing. She thought of her own mother and could see her now, in her hairnet and overalls, smoking a Marlboro. Her mother smoked Marlboros until they killed her. She'd operated a sheet metal press for a company that made anything out of sheet metal. Boxes for utilities mainly, containers for the military. She worked more or less until she died. Mary Ann wondered if her momma ever had the hot flashes, or ever woke up in the middle of the night scared she was dying, or got mad at herself for being so ridiculous. When Mary Ann gave birth and named her daughter Mary Jean, her momma didn't approve. "Too close to Mary Ann," she said flatly. "Too close to naming a man for his daddy. I ain't never known a man named Junior who turned out to be any damn good at all. It ruins 'em for some reason. Don't know why, it just does. And don't get me started on why anyone goes around by Something Something the Third. Don't get me started." Her momma fired up another Marlie and never spoke of naming daughters again. But Mary Ann always remembered that conversation. She was mad. "Jesus Momma," she'd said, "Don't speak about my baby that way." After some time, she could laugh the memory off. She wished Momma was around. Not for advice or anything, but just to be around.

She got to the Facility and went through the process — the bag from the convenience store got dumped out and sorted, then put back together — and walked on into the central meeting room where Mary Jean sat at a table like she always did the first Saturday of the month.

"Momma." Mary Jean looked like Peyton, only older. Same blue eyes, same braided hair. "Peyton not coming?"

"She'll come when she's ready," Mary Ann said, same as she did the first Saturday of every month. Mary Jean turned over one of the chocolate bars. She unwrapped the end and inhaled deeply through her nose. "Thanks Momma." She carefully rewrapped the bar and placed it with the others. When Mary Ann first started coming, she thought she should bring cigarettes. "No Momma," Mary Jean told her. "Well, maybe a little. But chocolate goes farther." Mary Ann admired that her daughter quit smoking. Tough place to quit. Mary Jean was five foot seven and weighed one-hundred-and-one pounds when she went in. That was the meth. Even in the Facility she hadn't gained much back. Mind you, Mary Ann's own momma was wiry skinny too, with a Marlie always on her lip. It must skip a generation, she thought. God Damn. The half hour passed. She showed photos of Peyton on her phone, and asked questions about Mary Jean's eating (*well*) and about meetings (*learning good coping skills, gonna stay clean forever.*)

"How's Jimmy?" her daughter asked.

"Same as always. Watching football. Wants his Slurpee," Mary Ann answered.

When she left the Facility, the leaves were drying on the trees, crumbling into dust in the air. August more than October. She turned off the A/C and rolled down the window and came back to the convenience store. She bought Jimmy's Slurpee and the last two copies of *Women's Holistic Health*. "It's a great issue," she told the clerk, who hadn't asked. "I'm giving them to friends. Maybe I'll leave one in my doctor's waiting room." She threw them in the garbage on the way out. With the sun on her face, the Slurpee felt good against her forehead. The sun and the wind made her feel she was inside a dream. She finished the Slurpee as she pulled up to the house.

Before she set her keys down, Jimmy hollered from the couch, "Did you get me a Slurpee?"

"Umm. Sorry. I forgot." Her mouth was still cold and sweet.

"No problem," he shouted, cheerful as always. "Tell you what. It's almost half time. Y'all wanna go into the bedroom and get yourself ready?"

She rolled her eyes.

"I can feel you rolling your eyes from here, sweet thing. Hey, even if I can't promise it'll be any good, I can promise you it won't drag on. Second half is coming up!' He laughed after that.

"Maybe next time, Mr. Romance," she yelled over the TV. "I gotta go back out again."

"What's that?" Jimmy hollered back.

"I forgot Peyton at the pool."

"You forgot?"

"I know. I know," said Mary Ann. "I must be gettin' old."

She sat on the bench in the entryway, too heavy all of a sudden and much too tired.

Jimmy came out. "You want me to go get her?"

"No, I'm all right. I can get your Slurpee, too."

He knelt down and faced her. "Mary Ann. Did you get any sleep last night?"

She leant and touched her forehead to his. "Somewhere between not much and none at all."

In that moment she could see Momma, her hand on her hip and a Marlie in the corner of her mouth. Standing there, not saying anything.

She closed her eyes. "You know, Jimmy, I wish you had met my momma. She never forgot anything. Ever. The last thing she said to me before she passed was, "I love you and your sister. You remember that. And remember to feed the cat."

"I wish I'd met her too. She sounded like some lady." Jimmy's voice had softened. "I do remember the cat. I may have missed your momma, but I did show up for the cat."

Mary Ann took his arm and pulled herself upright.

"That damn cat lived five more years after Momma passed, and it had to have been fourteen when it died. A lazy and spiteful creature if there ever was one."

Jimmy laughed. "You sure you don't want me to go get Peyton? It's no problem."

"No. I got it, Jimmy."

Mary Ann walked back out the door into sun coming down through the leaves, casting light and shadow in inscrutable patterns on the road like fish scales.

On Mountains and Menopause

JANE CAWTHORNE AND E. D. MORIN

E. D. MORIN: We've had some great conversations since starting this project. There were pieces we hoped we would get on certain topics, one of which was women who pursue sports in later life. We wanted to hear from and about women who were at the top of their game athletically. Or who felt physically and mentally liberated for the first time in their lives. Women who could devote their energies to higher physical pursuits to an extent that wasn't possible while devoted to a career and a family.

My sister Lou Morin, whose "Hidden Talents" appears in this anthology, expressed how her own experience confirmed this phenomenon: "On a practical level, there are certain pursuits that are incredibly hard to pull off during childrearing years. Crazy as it seems, I wasn't able to walk anywhere in the city for twelve years before my son entered junior high. And that's not even mountain climbing! Until then, in order to hold a job, I had to drive my son to and from school. I had to drive everywhere."

Somehow Jane, independently, you and I chose to pursue mountaineering when we were hovering around the fifty mark, right before our kids left home. There was something going on at that time. It was no coincidence, especially living near the Rockies as we both did then. I've noticed the recreational climbing world is populated with a significant number of women in their forties, fifties, and sixties. What do you make of that?

JANE CAWTHORNE: I can't call myself a climber, but it's true I got attracted to the sport in my late forties. I'd always been a hiker and wanted to get to places I hadn't been able to reach before — real wilderness. My own story is complicated by cancer. Was it recovering from cancer that made me want this? Or menopause? It is impossible to know and impossible to separate the two. But yes, there is something to what you are suggesting. Or maybe it is because women our age have a deep need to get away from people, to go somewhere more elemental where the usual restrictions and expectations don't apply.

E.D.: There's something universal going on here beyond mountains and climbing. Maybe we've played out our roles as baby-makers and child-minders, as peacemakers, as love objects even. Maybe we've secretly despised these roles, even as we celebrated, endured, or encouraged them. At this point, we needed to unlearn all that. Maybe it was time to raise some hell of our own, but on our own terms.

I recently watched *Pretty Faces*, an all-female ski film by Lynsey Dyer. There was something absolutely novel going on there. The film highlighted the usual aerial stunts and epic ski lines (these so-called pretty mountain faces) but in an exuberant, infectious way. No lone-king posturing here. Instead these women were enjoying being powerful together, in pairs, in trios, having silly badass fun. It was about the narrative, about female friendships. In one fell swoop Dyer, an accomplished mountain skier in her own right, managed to humanize the entire ski film genre. One of my all-time heroes, backcountry ski pioneer Marion Schaffer (still rocking the slopes in her sixties) even has a cameo.

This documentary gives me hope. I have seen the possibilities in person. My best backcountry ski days have been with women. One of my favourite alpine climbs was on a female only rope-team. It turns out menopausal women can hoot and holler and give high fives at the bottom of a ski run or at the top of a summit as loudly and exuberantly as anyone.

Maybe what I'm saying is we are not our mothers.

JANE: No, we are not our mothers. Well, I don't know about your mother, but my mother didn't know what to do with herself after her role of caregiver and wife was over. My father died just as the youngest (me) was leaving the nest. She spent the rest of her life in limbo, looking back. And it was a long life too. I always wanted her to do something else, but she didn't know what to do. It was hard to watch.

I think many of us face this question of what to do in this part of our lives. I still see many women return to their former roles. They become caregivers for their grandchildren. I realize how necessary this is. Times are tough and working parents need childcare. And grandparents love their grandkids and want to do it. But at the same time, I think it's kind of a shame that many women are encouraged into the same old role they've always had. Maybe they are grateful for it — better the devil you know. But for me, I want something new.

E.D.: My mother took up silversmithing in her fifties after years of illness. She still has quite the grip, even in her eighties. I am so proud of how she remade herself. She was able to carve out a second, creative life after children. But she is not an outdoorswoman, not by a long shot. Who knows? Maybe she might have been one, if not for the chronic pain she's suffered most of her life. And of course raising six kids! So I rarely talk about the things I do in the backcountry with her, because I fear it would stress her out too much. Story of our relationship. My mother worries about everything.

JANE: My mother worried about everything too. She worried about me on the simplest camping trips, so I used to keep my adventures from her. Her worried voice could really get into my head. But mountaineering helped me to break through the fear I was starting to feel. I could feel myself becoming tentative. I was feeling my frailty in a different way in my late forties, and I could see how fear could creep up on me and invade my psyche. I might fall. I might break my increasingly brittle bones. I didn't want to become a worrier. I didn't want to limit myself with fear.

Practically speaking, I faced a serious barrier to going into the wilderness. I was having random, excessive, impossible bleeding.

Terrible. I always had a sweater to tie around my waist, like a teenager. It took some time but with the help of my doctor, I finally found a solution that worked for me. Once I had that under control, I could go out in the wilderness again without being afraid of having a sudden pant-destroying flood.

E.D.: I agree, it's no fun having erratic periods at altitude with people you barely know. On a remote trail or on a glacier, there aren't many sanitary facilities. There may be an outhouse, but it'll be back at camp several kilometres away. Few men will admit how much harder we have to work as women, how many more steps it takes to live in our bodies, how much more paraphernalia we have to cart around. If you tell a man this, he'll probably stare blankly. Maybe he'll look away or change the subject or if he's decent he'll offer you dark chocolate. Most likely he'll set off down the trail at a gallop.

And it's even worse if you mention menopause.

JANE: Did you ever notice how *Freedom of the Hills* [the mountaineer's bible] doesn't talk about how to cope with menstruation? There are pages and pages about how to dispose of other bodily wastes but not blood. And blood is a real problem. Maybe that's why some women finally try wilderness adventures after menopause. For the first time, they don't have to worry about the blood.

E.D.: When you didn't find anything about menstruation in the mountaineer's bible, I went online and found women sharing their insights (http://andrewskurka.com/2013/female-hygiene-guide-tips). And sure enough one commenter said, "I can't say enough about post-menopausal backpacking."

JANE: So it's not just us who feel this way.

E.D.: No, it's not. My sister Lou says of our mountaineering pursuits, "So there's the bleeding and there's the papoose aspect [of carrying a backpack] to this life phase. Is it symbolic that you transitioned from being bound to your children, to binding yourself by choice with harness and rope to a mountain? I wonder."

JANE: I wonder too. I wonder if women in all kinds of different pursuits, sports or otherwise, would have a similar conversation. I bet they would. I wish we had received those kinds of submissions.

E.D.: It gets me thinking about women who are confronting poverty and how they feel about entering menopause. I've heard about women whose only access to a lavatory is a public facility, and how every time they need to use the toilet they fear being attacked. That's an entirely different realm of safety compared to the backcountry. I wish we had been able to solicit submissions from them. I wonder, do they see the end of bleeding as a blessing? Or maybe fear and anxiety never end. Maybe they transfer these fears to their daughters and nieces and granddaughters.

JANE: Of course, there are so many other topics we hoped to get submissions about, sports-related or otherwise. There is much more to be said and many more women to speak.

E.D.: Somehow we have to make space for ourselves. There is no reason why mountaineering, or any physical pursuit, can't be a space where women feel secure and invested. Where we put on a harness, tie onto a rope, and feel tethered.

JANE: Making this book together feels like that, like tying into a rope, tethering together.

THREE: UN/KNOWN

Evie's Massage Parlour

ROBERTA REES

I

That she reached menopause, my mother. That she reached menstruation.

That she survived, gave birth to four children she raised with ferocious big-hearted love.

Oxygen tubes up her nose in her little subsidized apartment where she cooks for anyone who looks hungry, tells bullies to fuck off, hangs a sign on her door, "Evie's Massage Parlour, Take Your Clothes Off Before You Enter."

II

Menopause began one-ovaried, surgically induced when she was thirty-seven. In the mountain village where we lived, broody mountains all around, the grey-gouged face of Turtle Mountain rising above town at the west end of Main Street, its ninety million tons of fractured limestone rubbling the valley of coal mining towns necklaced along the river.

Bellevue. The funny looks when we told people where we lived. An intense place, our Bellevue, forty years ago when my mother was thirty-seven — big thighed, bulgy muscled from pitching softball, hitting homeruns out of ballparks, running twelve machines at a cable winding factory up the valley — stopped on her way uptown to get our mail and run errands at the Seniors' Centre where they called her "Legs."

Stopped in the -30°F breath-snapping, constant wind, braced herself against the wall of a plumbing shop, a wave of heat igniting her, drenching her in dizzy sweat. "What the hell, what the goddamned hell."

"Menopause," the post-mistress told her as my mother whipped off her coat and scarf, a sensation of drowning, heart pounding, gasping for air.

"You're less of a woman now, no wonder your husband left you," another woman said when my father, my mother's shy handsome lover since their teens — two homeless youths longing for love and security — at thirty-five ran away from our home with a singer from his band, and they sang their way through the U.S. while my mother ran her twelve machines at the cable plant.

When she was working the night shift she hemorrhaged, blood poured through her clothes onto the cement floor between her machines, washed across the concrete and a man at the next bank of machines ran for towels, said he felt like he was going to pass out.

III

"Don't feel sorry for me," she says, flipping the tangled cord that tethers her to the oxygen machine constantly humming in the entrance to her apartment. "This is my life. It isn't who I am. I've had a good life."

I nod, take off my shirt, my bra, so she can massage my shoulders and back, the way she did when I was the baby she birthed at seventeen, the way she has my whole life. Look up at the photos of grandkids on her green walls, photos of her in Australia when she was fifty-five and taking what she called her "happy shot" to stop the spontaneous human combustion that would boil up, drench her with sweat and foul temper.

"I can't take hormones," I say, sweat beading my back under her skinny fingers, my heart starting that erratic thump-thump-thumping that quakes the bones, "migraines, risk of stroke."

"I worry about your migraines," she says, "your Auntie Mert died at fifty-one after a three-day migraine."

Wheeze enters her boned-down chest, the heavy wet cough coming up, slumping her forward, unable to breathe in or out, drowning in thick phlegm and so I sit silent, "Don't hover when I get like that," while she heaves and rocks and coughs and pants.

I focus on the photos of her on her fridge:

Robust and smiling, sometime in her forties, receiving first prize in a horseshoe pitching tournament.

In her ball uniform, head cocked, cocky grin, squinting into the sun, her face middle age proud.

Also at middle age in her blue flowered pie dress, the hundreds of pies she baked to sell at markets, entered into pie baking contests at summer fairs. Baked, packed, carried hundreds of pies.

On a painting ladder, that meditative gaze when she got up in the middle of the night, took her tools to whatever home or business or construction site she was contracting to, spent nights and days getting the job right and loving the dance of challenge and skill, providing for herself after my father — who came home from his singing spree months after he left, unable to forgive himself — died at fifty, and my mother did forgive, loved and nursed him for two agonizing years. Construction chemicals poisoning her unprotected lungs.

On a horse in Australia where she got a job guiding tourists on horseback through the rainforest, her back straight, easy and alert on her horse, a feather in the band of her Akubra hat pulled low over her brow.

A photo of her we had enlarged for her seventy-fifth birthday — fifteen, athletic arms, legs, gabardine cowboy pants, cowboy hat, laughing in the sun.

And finally the phlegm spews from her body into a Kleenex and she sits back, eyes watering, sucks in. "It's bullshit to let anyone make you think you become invisible or stupid just because you don't have periods or much pubic hair," and we start to laugh, laugh until we cry and she starts choking again at the joke between us — the time she asked me to get slimmer "piss pads" for her because the sticky strip on the wide ones got caught in her hair.

"How did it get all the way up to your head," I'd asked on the phone, and the next day she greeted me at her apartment door with a bladder-leak pad twisted into a bow over her ear.

"I have my burning paid for," she says when she catches her breath.

"We're born to die," she pats my shoulder, "the moment we're born we're going to die. It's what we do in between that matters."

IV

The sheer guts it takes for her to walk the length of the apartment hall, oxygen tank over her shoulder, leg muscles atrophied, shape of her bones, her knees, through her pants. Shoulders hitched, curve of ribs, sheer effort of breathing.

To the car, into our favourite lunch place — a fish restaurant. Wind stealing what breath she has.

Seated by the time I park the car, joking with the waitress. "One of the best jobs I ever had," she says of her years of waiting tables, short order cooking, when she was a fifteen-year-old living on her own and the handsome jockey from the thoroughbred track came into the Stampede Grill. When she was seventeen and pregnant with me, but didn't know why she kept throwing up.

And through those eighteen years of hot sweats and happy shots — when my father was on strike at the strip mine where he worked and my mother took a job at a ski hill cooking thousands of hamburgers, cabbage rolls, eggs, and bacon. And during the time my father was a runaway and she left the cable plant, the job she took waiting tables and cooking in one of the other towns in the valley where everyone knew her husband had run away, and she laughed and joked, delivered food to tables, told a man making a sexist comment to fuck off, got fired and rehired in five minutes.

"But didn't you feel invisible or that you had a lack of power with menopause," I ask her.

"I wouldn't let anyone make me feel invisible," she says, flipping her oxygen cord, "You don't survive what I survived and let anyone make you think you're invisible just because you have your uterus removed or your hormones change."

V

The kinds of invisibility that offer refuge.

The kinds that can kill us.

The summer my sister turned eleven and her breasts grew larger than mine and our mother's, and kept growing.

The shape girls and women were told we should want. Large breasts. Slim hips and legs.

"Slut," the boys on Main hissed when my sister had to pass them on her way to the bus stop.

"Slut," in the hallways at school, and no one stopped them.

Adult men leered at her. In the arena, in the café, on the streets of our village.

The layers of clothing she started wearing.

The boy who cornered her in the dark, shoved her to the ground, clamped a hand over her mouth and nose, jammed his forearm into her windpipe, "You want this as much as I do, cunt, tell and I'll kill you."

"Slut," the boys hissed in all the hallways and streets, "Cunt, two-bit whore. Jump her, fuck her."

The man at a party in the city she escaped to, his hand reaching for her breast, "Are they real?" His offence when she walked away, "I was giving you a compliment, bitch."

The physician in the long hospital corridor where she had to pass him every day on her way to work, his eyes locked on her breasts.

"Teach your breasts ventriloquism," I suggested, "Have them say 'get your fucking eyes off me,' or stare at his crotch the whole length of the hallway."

The way he squirmed, turned and faced the wall, scrabbled past.

The prying hands, words, leering eyes of so many men.

Her first mammary reduction at nineteen. "Smaller," she told the surgeon after he presented the size he envisioned for her, explained the risks and the procedure — anaesthetic, slice of knife, removal of nipples, removal of tissue, reattachment of her nipples, possibility of lost sensation.

"Smaller," she said.

The look in her eyes when the nurse removed the bloodied bandages and she looked down at her wounded breasts. "He didn't listen to me."

VI

"Exposed," she said years later, "violated" about the decades of men's eyes and hands and words, and the boy who raped her got married, had kids, walks around our village, the same village my sister gets nauseated driving into.

"Who's going to believe me," she says after her second reduction, her surgical menopause at forty-one, "I thought it was my fault, that somehow I deserved it."

Layers of clothing, body fat.

"If I tell now, who gets hurt — his wife and kids."

VII

"Menopause," her doctor says when my sister goes to see her about the drenching night sweats, pounding heart that makes her bed shake, dizziness that makes her afraid to walk, extreme fatigue.

"But I've been through that, after the hysterectomy. This is different."

"Anxiety," the doctor says, writes a prescription for anti-depressants, group therapy.

And my sister keeps going back. "I can't sleep my heart is pounding so hard, I'm drowning in sweat. I feel like I'm going to have a heart attack."

Prescription for an additional anti-depressant.

"My heart is pounding out of my chest, I've been fainting."

"You didn't really faint. You just thought you did."

"There's a guy with anger issues in group therapy," she tells me on the phone, "He loses it — shouts, gets physically aggressive."

"I can't be in that group," she tells the psychologist, her doctor,

"I was raped at fifteen."

"You have to work through it so you're not so easily triggered."

"I'm not the one who needs to work through his anger."

"You have to self-advocate to get better."

"I can't be in there with him."

"Non-compliant," the psychologist says, and the doctor writes on my sister's chart.

My sister who did hundreds of hours of sweat equity labour on her Habitat for Humanity house, aced physiology and kinesiology classes, hiked in the mountains with our family, moved a ton of sod in one day, is raising two amazing daughters as a single parent.

"What about these bruises," she asks her doctor and starts to raise her shirt to show her doctor the massive bruise covering half her torso. "What about this rash on my stomach?"

"It's okay, I don't need to see." More drugs, more discussion of mood, therapy.

"Could this be lymphoma," my sister asks, "I'm forty-eight, our father died of lymphoma at fifty; he had night sweats and fainting."

"Anxiety. Depression," the doctor writes in my sister's chart. And never runs a blood test.

"Anxiety attack," the paramedic says when he comes to her friend's house where her friend is holding my sister on the bed.

"Heart attack," they say in the back of the speeding ambulance where they test for troponin in her blood.

"I'm not recovering, I'm trembling, fainting," she tells the head of cardio rehab when she's out of hospital.

And he sends her to a psychiatrist. "Your symptoms aren't depression," the psychiatrist says after several sessions and blood tests, "there's something physically wrong. You need to go back to your doctor."

"How did this happen," she says after the diagnosis — Stage IV Lymphoma — "Why wasn't I heard?"

VIII

"Why am I still not being heard," she asks after the car accident halfway through chemo, caused by the other driver, that totals her car, slams her into the steering wheel, damages her shoulder, her chest, knees, jaw.

The doctor she sees who puts up his hand for three years when she keeps coming back to ask for an investigation into her continued pain, keeps asking her about her mood.

The locum who asks, "If I could wave a magic wand, what one issue would you choose?"

IX

"Rape culture," I say to a friend, "We're finally talking about it, we're finally being heard."

"You're more hopeful than I am," she says.

"Maybe," I say.

X

All the girls and women who never make it to menopause.

"He looks like the man who raped me," my mother says when she sees the photo in the book about Russell Williams, the leader of an air force base who tortured and murdered two vibrant young women, one a flight attendant on "his" base.

"I've been having flashbacks," she says when she hears the news of the six-year-old girl raped and beaten beyond recognition, the fifteen-year-old First Nations girl raped and beaten, dumped into the Assiniboine River. "I want to go hold them, tell them it wasn't their fault."

XI

What the elderly woman in 1948 said to the little girl on her doorstep — half naked, battered and bitten, bleeding, trembling.

Wrapped her in a quilt, held her, "You did nothing wrong, you did not deserve this." Rocked her, called the police, "Send the woman officer."

The woman officer who held the girl in the police car, "You did nothing wrong," miles through the city to the little girl's clapboard house in the inner-city warehouse district, the house the girl had left hours earlier to go fetch her father from the bar, her mother too sick with lung disease to get up, the other seven kids somewhere else.

Was passing Lowney's warehouse two doors down when a man stepped out of the shadows, "Hey, little girl, anyone ever tell you that you look like Shirley Temple," locked her in a choke-hold before she could answer, clamped his other hand over her mouth and nose, dragged her miles through town, kicking and trying to breathe, not one person she knew in their warehouse district out on the street.

"My daughter," he told strangers they passed, "I'm taking her home," his hand cutting off her breath.

"Famous," he said when he pulled her into the bushes beside the river miles from home, "I'll make you famous."

"Famous as Shirley Temple," and he got off her to find a rock and the girl heard her mother call her name, staggered half-conscious to her feet, into the river, swam even though she couldn't swim, the man somewhere behind her, frantic up the far riverbank, across the road, banging on doors until the elderly woman opened her door.

"You did nothing wrong," her mother said, black circles around her eyes from not being able to breathe, "that man is evil," held her daughter crazed with fear and hurt while the doctors examined her and the girl heard them say, "She's so damaged inside, she'll never be able to have kids." Took her trembling daughter into bed with her because the girl couldn't be around any male, not even her brothers.

Died three weeks later — violent eruption of her aorta and the little girl thought she'd killed her mother.

Wanted to die, sat catatonic on the street outside the funeral home, in the court where she had to testify against the man who aimed his finger at her like a gun, "When I'm out in five, kid, I'll hunt you down, I'll find you, I'll make you famous."

XII

"I worry about you writing about stuff like this," a woman says to me after a book-club discussion of my last book, "There's so much dark stuff, I worry about your mental health."

She is a stranger to me; her eyes are kind.

"Your mother shouldn't talk about stuff like that," someone said to me when I was in high school, "What happened to her as a kid, your dad running away, hot flashes — people don't want to hear stuff like that."

XIII

"Don't say I died," my mother says, boned down scrawny. "Because I didn't. Not yet."

"Do you think you spoke up more during or after menopause," I ask her and my sister when I show them what I've written.

My mother rolls her gaunt shoulders, cocks her head, "I always spoke up for myself. If that didn't work, I used my fists."

The three of us bust out laughing.

"What about you," I ask my sister.

"A little bit," she says, "Not during, but after."

"Do you have anything else you'd want to say about menopause?"

"Yup — my hat goes off to women."

Hidden Talents

LOU MORIN

I finally solved the riddle of my singular talent several hours after the international chess master left my office. Meeting under the pretence of discussing his rejected manuscript, he fixed himself in the chair opposite mine and wouldn't budge unless I offered him a publishing job — one that hadn't been advertised and didn't even exist. He seemed agitated and angry, desperate even. Too polite to ask him to leave, I struggled with the exchange, feeling increasingly distressed as the hour passed.

When he ran out of moves, my opponent resigned the game and left my office. A quick check-in with Google revealed the man's stature in the chess world. As I write this now, I realize how difficult it must have been for this brilliant player and his pride, and why he felt he had to exhaust every move before conceding. He'd suffered a double loss — the editorial board had declined his life story *and* he hadn't found the job he sought. And I, unwittingly, had beaten a world master.

Later that day, having reclaimed my safe space and found solace in chocolate, I had a revelation. My visitor's departure had left a strong odour that followed me home and lasted well into evening. Alien, acrid, and unnerving, it directed my attention like an alarm. "I can smell crazy people!" I announced to my family.

When I was thirty-two, I lost my sense of smell and some of my vision following the surgical removal of a growth on my pituitary gland. Once a restaurant pastry cook, I could no longer detect familiar odours or taste many foods. Gone in seven hours was my scent taxonomy, including the splendid fragrances of loved ones, newborns, herbs of any kind, stinky cheese, frangipane, soil after rain, and newly-printed books. Suffering from anosmia, the inability to smell, meant not only grieving the loss of these treasured scents, but also the associated memories and emotions they evoked.

In the beginning, I perceived phantom odours. Phantosmia can occur after the olfactory system is disconnected. I once enjoyed the smell of roast turkey for hours, making everything I ate that day taste like Thanksgiving. In this way, I briefly enjoyed aromatic hallucinations, then nothing at all. My world was abruptly deodorized. Or so I thought.

Grateful to have survived brain surgery, I chose to focus on what I'd gained, rather than what I'd lost. I allowed my love of science to pilot this unexpected development — this corporeal *terra incognita* — and treated it like an experiment. As a child, I'd treasured a literary relic that somehow made its way into my possession and still lives on my bookshelf: Tom Tit's *La science amusante* (Paris, 1906). I remember devouring its archaic text and surrealist engravings that described wacky DIY physics projects, all deliciously deckle-bound in worn leather and faded marbled paper. I could picture myself blowing concentric soap bubbles and fearlessly defying gravity with looped paper. Now, as an adult facing a perplexing health challenge, I indulged these childhood aspirations. My dream of becoming a mad scientist was taking shape, or scent, or whatever. I hadn't quite figured it out at that point.

But the chemistry set and microscope of my elementary years would soon be replaced by another unique set of metrics when my newly inodorous world revealed itself to be otherwise. With the usual cacophonous range of smells stripped away, I'd somehow gained the ability to detect physiological clues normally hidden by ambient aromas. A limbic faculty, my sixth sense, detected a seemingly random odour that could last for hours, giving me pause to question its purpose. This new scent was unlike any I'd known. Chemical and somewhat unpleasant, it left me feeling alert, sometimes fearful, and it just smelled ... wrong.

The distinctive odour surfaced intermittently, during odd social exchanges, maybe four times a year. I didn't keep track back then. There was the frightening time a man knocked on my door late one night looking for a party down the block, then reappeared an hour later staring through the window. The encounter left me with a stifling sense of fear and that chemical, unpleasant scent. I was so shaken, I left and slept at a friend's house. The alarm scent stayed with me until morning. I filed away this and other such incidents as somehow related to my long-dormant lizard brain. My twenty-first century thinking brain didn't as yet know how to catalogue them.

Then, I had the meeting with the chess player and finally connected the mysterious odour with intense emotional distress. I was forty-six, and only starting to truly know myself. This was indeed a personal revelation: I was an olfactive savant.

I see it as no coincidence that I made this discovery in my middle years. Cultural conversation tends to focus on the often-onerous physical and emotional shifts brought on by menopause, framing this significant transition as an affliction. But I've also read that mid-life hormonal upheaval triggers a rewiring of the female brain, bringing gifts of heightened intuition, the ability to place ourselves first, and the resolve to stop putting up with crap. For me, this meant gaining the insight, clarity, and grit needed to journey deeper into my sensory conundrum, to embrace my inner scientist, and to realize I should have kicked the damn chess master out of my office long before he left.

Discovery led to inquiry, the next leg of my journey. How could I pick up these atypical odours when I couldn't detect typical ones? Was there anything else I could smell that others couldn't? Would my "normal" olfactory system eventually return? And if it did, would I lose this new superpower — my supersonic feelings radar? I turned to literature for answers. I never thought to ask a doctor, as I didn't expect them to engage in a conversation about crazy smells and phantom odours. Instead, I saw an opportunity to be both examiner *and* specimen. Like daring Tom Tit, I would search for answers through a series of do-it-myself scientific trials.

I found I was far from alone. Millions of people across the world suffer from olfactive dysfunction due to surgery like mine, or to congenital conditions, head trauma, sinus infections, allergies, virus, or disease. I read on, sorting through the symptoms of anosmia, phantosmia, parosmia, troposmia, and dysosmia. But my particular type of "osmia," one that signalled emotional upheaval, was not mentioned in scholarly articles or online discussions. Here, I *was* on my own.

Until recently, smell has been the outlier of the senses. Science is only now beginning to unravel its workings. As new interdisciplinary taste and smell clinics are established across Europe and the U.S. to advance the study of the two chemical senses, researchers are finding that our olfactory ecology is more powerful and complex than previously believed. Paleontologists posit that people "smelled their way to bigger brains," driving changes in the temporal lobes, the area of the brain where smell is processed. These changes evolved into an ingenious interpersonal communication system used today to navigate social life.

On the broadcasting side, we emit two kinds of sweat — the one physical, the other emotional. This second, lesser-known type of sweat serves as a situational flag, releasing airborne chemical signals that transmit covert, often emotional, information between people. These specialized molecules, *my* mysterious alarm scent, make up what scientists term "social odours," commonly known as pheromones. Corollary to these transmitted chemosignals is an accessory olfactory system that detects and processes them. When I lost my primary sense of smell, this secondary system may have stepped up, helping me chart the world on a different level — like taking a sudden exit from a predictable trajectory onto a hidden freeway of complex signals.

My younger scientist self would have been pleased. Having pieced together the fifteen-year puzzle of my altered nose, I began to channel my newfound skill. Validation came one day when I suddenly picked up the stress scent during a professional exchange with a new colleague. I guessed that one of us was in a panic, and I knew it wasn't me. Moments later, my co-worker's distress spilled out as he professed his marriage was breaking up, and he asked me for advice. My emotional radar was on the nose. It was an epiphany! I began to see my impairment as a gift that invited a deeper connection with the world. And I accepted that I would pass through life smelling the emotional ripples in my environment.

As a secret smelling agent, I've come to know when a store manager's tolerance is stretched beyond its limits on an insanely chaotic opening day, when a colleague is suffering unduly from bullying, when someone sleeping beside me is having a nightmare. If I share the tale of my hidden talent, my *phenomenose*, with others, I do so cautiously. "Have you smelled it on me?" they'll ask, worried their body odour might betray their secrets. Which leaves me wondering if most people walk around questioning their own sanity. In an imagined scenario I picture myself busking on a street corner where I take a deep whiff of my customers before handing them a *yea* or *nay* mental health report card, like Charlie Brown's Lucy at her psychiatric help booth. "THE MAD SCIENTIST IS IN."

Through all of this, my old sense of smell has started to drift in and out of my olfactory field like an elusive target, surprising me now and then with a recognizable odour. This happens more often of late, giving me hope it might stay permanently. I've read that nerves can regenerate. Over the past weeks, summer odours — chlorine rising off a fountain, sweaty teenagers, freshly cut grass, the bottom of a drained coffee cup — have brought me brief and unexpected pleasure. I dare not hope too hard.

Periodically, I step back as lead scientist and allow others to direct this experiment. Twice, my health developments have stumped the specialists: first when a second tumour was found on my pituitary, then when the gland stopped functioning many years after surgery. Bi-annual MRIs scan my skull for possible tumour re-growth, annual visual field tests scope my damaged optical nerves, and routine visits with concerned endocrinologists monitor my limping endocrine system. But the self-directed sensory study continues. While some of my earlier questions remain unanswered, new ones have joined the queue. I wonder how technology has affected our senses. Will our dependence on digital pings dumb us down, leaving humans with sensory deficit disorder? Will evolution reclaim what it gave us by conceding to our reliance on these electronic communication systems? Are there others out there who can single out social odours?

And so, after twenty years of trials, I've decided to offer myself up to science. By approaching the research community and offering myself as a subject, I'll have a better chance of finding answers, opening up new paths to explore and helping others. With this mission in mind, I've collected the names of top international chemosensory scientists. I've composed and re-composed inquiries to two of them. Holding the key to the next turn in my fantastic inner voyage, the e-mails sit in my Draft folder waiting for me to click Send.

I've come a ways. Through pluck, chance, strategy, and blunder, I've shielded my queen piece from perilous attacks, taking out a dark knight and a rook or two along the way. I'm ready to make the next move, to learn as much as I can about the wonderfully enigmatic workings of my temporal lobes, and to take the next step. This will be my end game.

Drenched

LEANNA MCLENNAN

For two years, I woke up every night drenched in sweat. At the time, I lived in a rundown apartment on the top floor of a converted house so I could afford to rent an art studio. I pictured the retail clerk, who controlled the thermostat downstairs and dreamed of being a fashion stylist, walking around in a tank top.

I mean, it's winter. Put on a sweater.

When my period stopped, suddenly it wasn't so hot.

You're lucky, I can't wait to not have to worry about my period.

I liked the viscous consistency of my blood and that its monthly return meant that my body was cleansing. I liked having that connection with other women.

But I didn't like the two days before my period when I felt that no one loved me. Nor did I like having to lie in a hot bathtub to counter the waves of cramps and painful memories.

When I told my doctor that I felt sad, she referred me to a young male psychiatrist, who thanked her for sending him, "this very interesting thirty-eight-year-old patient." His diagnosis: I didn't suffer from depression but PMS. Still, he recommended that I take Prozac.

After this, I tracked my moods and realized that I felt agonizingly sad for only two days a month. Each time the sadness returned, I knew it would be with me for only two days, so I bought a box of tissues, a *Vogue* magazine, and a chocolate bar. Then I stayed home, ate bonbons, admired fancy clothes, and cried until my period arrived and the emotional pain became physical.

When I complained about lying in a hot bathtub enduring waves of emotional and physical pain, my naturopath said, "It's a gift, an opportunity to see what's really upsetting you and to not repress it."

I thought of her words as I lay in the bathtub and later curled into a fetal position on the bathroom floor. Then I let go of those painful feelings.

You need a menstrual hut?

"Your aforementioned request will be duly considered in relation to the specified regulations and directed to the appropriate channels," my friend the office manager wrote in reply to my e-mail request.

No menstrual hut was provided, but I enjoyed imagining a moss-filled room at the university where women could meet and bleed.

The next week while I was teaching, I put my feet up on the table, leaned back, and said, "I have to put my feet up so I don't get menstrual cramps...and if I can't say this in a feminist theory class, where can I say it?"

Maybe I'd said too much.

Don't worry, everything will dry out and your eggs will shrivel up.

The doctor in her late twenties smiled sweetly, confirmed I was post-menopausal, and said not to worry, most women didn't miss their periods.

I walked home, through streets lined with Victorian houses, toward my apartment on a busy street on the edge of a quiet neighbourhood, the renter's block. I imagined my tubes withering, like a snake's shed skin, a thin trace of myself inside me.

After my period stopped, my vagina got so dry that one winter afternoon when I was walking down the street, I could feel the sides rubbing against each other.

I added more oils to my diet and put Vitamin E capsules in my vagina every other day, but I didn't like what they did to my smell. I tried coconut oil instead, but it melted as I put it in.

After menopause, the hymenal ring loses its elasticity, and it can be uncomfortable to have sex. I asked my doctor about using estrogen cream. She thought it was a good idea, but my naturopath wasn't so sure.

You're lucky, you don't have to worry about getting pregnant now.

In my late thirties, I went to a gynecologist because I didn't think I should be experiencing such intense menstrual pain. An ultrasound revealed that I likely had endometriosis, and an x-ray showed that my tubes were blocked.

"You can't have children," the gynecologist said. "Your generation was told you could have it all, that you could have careers and have children later in life. You hear about women who get pregnant after forty, but what you don't hear about is how much work it took for them to conceive. Women who really want children should have them before the age of thirty-five."

When I asked about in vitro fertilization, she said, "You could try, but in a study done by a clinic in Boston, the success rate for in vitro fertilization for women over forty was zero."

"Don't date her for these last few years when she can still have children if you're not serious," a woman had told my boyfriend.

"I don't have more time. I need to try this now, or I'll lose my chance," I told him after I visited the gynecologist.

But he wasn't ready to have that conversation, and the relationship ended shortly after that.

I wept, longing for the sleepless nights about which my friends complained, for a baby's cries to interrupt my sleep, for tiny arms to reach up for me.

Later, at a women's gathering, I squeezed into a crowded room and sat between two young women, our knees touching.

When our life-giving force was celebrated, I quietly grieved.

Really? I was glad to be done with that.

Many women speak of their period becoming irregular, or stopping for six months and coming back. But mine just stopped one day and never returned. If I had known that it would be the last one, I would have thrown a party. I would have spent more time looking at the glob floating in the water, like paint mixed to a perfect shade of red. I would have held my belly and felt the blood flowing under the surface, and said a prayer.

Wow! You don't look like you've gone through menopause.

At first, I accepted it as a compliment. Then I wondered, what does post-menopause look like?

If you had asked me when I was in my twenties, I wouldn't have imagined that being post-menopausal would mean that I would sell my belongings, move across the country to live by the ocean, and become a dancer.

Now, as I dance, I connect with others. We begin slowly, moving together on the wooden floor in the dance studio, flowing to a gentle wave in the music. We dance alone. We dance together. A woman joins me and we leap like teenagers. A young man gives me a warm hug. A woman in her seventies dances past, palms up. The dance builds to a crescendo before we meet again in stillness. Sometimes I weep. Sometimes I am elated, joyful. I hold my belly and say a silent prayer.

Pressed On

CAROL KAVANAGH

I sailed her close to the wind,
trimmed her tight, ran her hard
until I got the best out of her.
After she turned fifty —
a mutiny. Complaints:
insomnia as persistent
as the halyard's hollow
clang in the dark. Doldrums,
blinding sun, and flashing heat.

Find a port, she said
where we can rest, do repairs,
take on supplies. She warned
of our demise if I didn't take heed.
And, I didn't. I pressed her on.

Midnight Flit

TARYN THOMSON

I almost wrote this at three am. These days my body turns into an oven, and I wake on fire, damp and hot. All the stuff that weighs on me keeps my mind churning for a good while before I sleep again. I have been thinking about happiness lately and where it has gone. Not the "I just ate a delicious ice cream cone" kind of happiness, but that contented, settled alignment I have felt before. There is a stillness in this quality of happiness — a steadiness — a certainty. I realize this flavour of happiness cannot happen without a certain amount of freedom: the type of freedom I no longer have. The first time I felt truly free was after a four-month stint in Tel Aviv working as a nanny. I was nineteen years old. It was the job from hell and, although I was excited to be exploring Israel on my days off, I was miserable. One day my employer read my diary and I was so angry I decided to do a midnight flit. The escape was exciting. I packed secretly and slipped away, and I had a strange evening with some stoned Israeli soldiers and didn't call home. Unfortunately, my employer did. She told my poor parents I had "run off with an Arab." After a few nights in a Tel Aviv hostel, I took the bus down to Eilat, which is the resort town in Israel. In the hostel there, I met an amazing older woman who had just returned from India where she'd worked in Mother Teresa's charity. I had been feeling off-kilter — panicked about up and leaving my job like that, worried about money and about being in a war-torn country virtually alone. She went through my backpack with me, the one I had overstuffed back home in Vancouver, and she urged me to pare it down. Around her, I felt grounded. My fear shifted, and I realized that I was completely free. The world opened up as a great possibility and a question mark. Nobody knew where I was; I was not expected anywhere. I had no responsibilities. All I had was a backpack and my savings. All that was before me was choice and adventure. Choice and adventure — both feel lacking in my life these days. Maybe these night sweats are my body's battle cry. Rise up, she calls. Leave the dishes and the teenagers and the career and cat and lawn and neighbours and get the fuck out. Choice. Adventure. Freedom.

Ugly Duckling Syndrome

CAROLYN GAGE

What if it turned out that our problems as women were much simpler than we thought? What if much of the bewildering — and proliferating — array of seemingly unrelated symptoms and pathologies that afflict women could be viewed as the effect of one single syndrome? And what if that syndrome had a single cause: heteropatriarchy? A staunch reductionist, I am intrigued by the possibility, and in the interests of furthering this line of inquiry, I propose a name for this phenomenon: The Ugly Duckling Syndrome.

As you probably remember, in the fairy tale the Ugly Duckling was tormented by her so-called peers for being different, until the happy day when she discovered that she was really a swan and not a duck at all. In other words, her "differences" were normal and she could stop beating up on herself for not fitting in.

In my own experience, the Ugly Duckling Syndrome has provided an explanation for many of my "maladjustments." First and foremost, I am a lesbian, and although I lived as a heterosexual for many years, I believe I have always been a lesbian. My earlier relationships with men were wildly dissociative. And all the time I kept wondering what was wrong with me. In retrospect, I am proudest of the behaviours that caused me shame and embarrassment as a heterosexual. These "aberrant" behaviours were bearing witness to my swaniness, my lesbianism.

I had a terrible time with periods, hating my body and hating my womanhood. This was because duck culture doesn't make allowances for swan cycles. My moon time was a nuisance, a time when my body would exercise a will of its own and when I would have to fight it, drug it, or surrender to it.

Duck culture is linear, based on a definition of progress as steady accretion. Swan culture is cyclical, spiralling. We move forward in rhythmic circling motions that seem to double back to the beginning periodically. Our bloods ebb and flow, our possessions ebb and flow, our relationships ebb and flow. We adopt a grace about our losses and our gains, knowing that the process, not the results, is the focus. Because we live in spirals, not lines, we move in a third dimension and our progress is manifest in upward motion, rather than in forward or backward lines on the material plane.

Not only does duck culture violate the swan need for moon time withdrawal, but it also does not allow for adjustment to different seasons, climates, or weather conditions. In fact, duck culture has even pathologized the natural tendency of most life forms to slow down in winter! The duck name for this evolutionary adaptation is "Seasonal Affective Disorder!"

Linear duck culture also pathologizes grief, rage, and depression, all of which are necessary circling-back flight patterns essential to swan reconnaissance.

At thirty-six, I developed Chronic Fatigue Immune Deficiency Syndrome. In recovering from this devastating illness, I have had to study up on swan nutrition because, for most of my life, my eating habits reflected duck culture. I also had to notice that duck activities were meaningless and draining to me as a swan, sapping my will to live. I learned that I had been taught social patterns that invited victimization by ducks. I have had to train in swan self-defence. If my natural instincts about territory, environment, and feeding had not been so severely disrupted by exile from my native culture and by a resocialization process that amounted to brainwashing, I am convinced that I never would have contracted the disease.

And now here I am, facing menopause. The "symptoms" look suspiciously familiar: depression, mood swings, irritability, crying jags, suicidality, panic attacks, hypersensitivity, splitting headaches, fatigue, sleep disturbances. Are these really the effects of natural hormonal changes (proof of our ugly duckdom!), or are these traumatic responses to a sudden paradigm shift, as the body throws off the last constraints of an artificially imposed identity?

Could these disorders more accurately be termed the symptoms of captivity? Of exile from a beloved homeland? Of inability to protect or support one's children or one's art? Of identification with other forms of life that are being wiped out? Responses to forced labour? Repressed knowledge of trauma? Systemic poisoning? Pain of reintegrating parts of oneself that have been split off? The agony of remembering the unthinkable? The backlash of terror for breaking a taboo?

Menopause, as I see it, is not so much "The Change" as it is the "End of Denial." For better or worse, at menopause, it is no longer possible to believe that one is a duck. Depending on one's relationship to swanhood, menopause can either be a time of intense disorientation or of profound homecoming.

As lesbians, we began our journey with our coming out. Those same tools that enabled us to resist the institutions of compulsory heterosexuality will stand us in good stead as we sort through the myths and lies about menopause. And who knows? Maybe death, too, is just a final throe of the Ugly Duckling Syndrome.

Icing on the Cake

RACHEL WILLIAMS

The picture of my mother, father, and I was taken in the heart of
the South at my first wedding in June 1990. I am nineteen and
my mother is forty-six — only four years older than I am today.
My mother is wearing a peach taffeta cocktail dress and I look
like an upside down muffin made of white Italian silk covered in

seed pearl sprinkles. We are over-made, over-sprayed extras from *Designing Women*.

My father, present and relaxed, is oblivious to the undercurrent of feminine turmoil and wears a crooked, confident smile. My mother frowns and looks beyond the lens of the camera. Clearly, she would rather be doing something other than posing for Mr. Mizelle who is the only photographer in our tiny town of ten thousand. Mr. Mizelle wears slacks and white socks with his black shoes, and he still wears a pompadour. His son Mike was the first boy I ever French-kissed. He is not the boy I am marrying, but he is at the wedding like everyone else I have ever dated or known.

My face is plastered with a smile that does not engage the muscles around my eyes. I didn't want to get married. In February, I had tried to call it off. We were in the car and my fiancé was nonplussed as he stopped and started on the jammed freeway. He told me to keep the ring and think about it. I looked out the window and counted the orange traffic drums in the stifling silence. My finger felt like it was swelling around the white and gold filigree engagement ring, a treasured antique in his family. No amount of soapy water would ever help me get it off again. He knew that I would give in and marry him if he waited me out. He knew my resistance would pass. He was right. In the end, my need to make everyone happy overruled my gut-wrenching, sweaty-sheets-in-the-middle-of-the-night fear that I was doing the wrong thing. He was a nice guy after all. What more did I want?

Twenty minutes before the photograph was taken, my mother had been having a meltdown over hatpins and some ham biscuits that had not arrived at the reception on time. The annoyance is still on her face. Little did we know, she was in her first month of full-blown menopause. Now, twenty-three years later, I am perimenopausal and I recognize my mother's struggle.

The women on my maternal side start their periods late and stop bleeding early. My aunt was in menopause at thirty-eight. Our hair greys prematurely and we all get a "cute" little bulge right below our belly buttons. The only upside is that we become voluptuous. We finally grow the bosoms we had always tried to fake with padding and underwire. Our hips begin to resemble pumpkins. We look for undergarments with Lycra panels stitched in the front and support hose with built-in girdles. The extra weight that comes with menopause gives us a swagger that looks best in low heels and belted full skirts with low cut tops, the kind of outfit that square dancers on *Hee Haw* wear.

My mother's worst moment with me happened the previous September before my wedding. I had called her from my crappy apartment during my freshman year to explain that I might not return home from college until Thanksgiving. There was a long pause. I listened to the static as I twisted the telephone cord waiting for her response. I examined the peeling plaster ceiling. I could feel her rage building through the receiver. She drew in a long breath and then unleashed a blast of hysteria the likes of which I had never witnessed while I was living under her roof. It culminated in, "You are never coming home again, are you?" This shrill, guilt-laden, grief-stricken accusation was my mother's way of saying she missed me. It was her way of saying I was ungrateful.

Looking back, I realize my mother had been slowly unraveling since my first year of high school. She never slept. She was a bundle of nervous energy. She developed acne. She dismissively attributed her symptoms to too much caffeine or red wine. During these years, my father would do anything to avoid the passive-aggressive torrent of anguish and anxiety that had become my mother. He initiated a new tradition of month-long camping trips, and when he was home, he spent his Saturdays sailing his little boat up and down the river and working in the garden. My brother, the good child, had already fled to college. And I made my parents' life hell. I took some pleasure in heightening my mother's emotional state on a daily basis by letting her know, with the mouth of a sailor, that I felt tortured by her constant maternal scrutiny.

I know now that at the wedding, there was more bothering my mother than hatpins and ham. There were the usual crushing pressures of hosting a wedding, but added to this was our "mixed" marriage. We were from St. Peter's, the Episcopal church that was opened in 1822 and remained active thanks to old money and the pecking order that is pervasive in small towns. But I was marrying into Baptists — the old-fashioned kind of Baptists who do not drink and expect their wives to obey them. And I had not finished college yet.

But there was still one more issue, one I didn't learn about until years later, when my mother confessed that on the day of my wedding, she thought she was pregnant. I don't know when her period actually stopped. But I do know that on the day I got married she had chosen the implausible idea of pregnancy at forty-six over the plausible idea she had finally entered menopause. Magical thinking was one of my mother's special skills.

My conception in 1972 had been an accident. My mother, a trained nurse, mistook breastfeeding for birth control. I can't believe that she trusted this bit of family planning folklore. Her first baby, my brother, was only nine months old when I was conceived. Then or now, she would have had one choice. My father was pro-life. Only a year before, he had tried to convince her to join his empty-nest scheme of adopting a child from Korea. He would have welcomed another child.

Perhaps she was so angry after my wedding and after learning the truth, because she felt her uterus had betrayed her. Once again, she'd fallen victim to her body's deception. She was no longer fertile. Her children had left. She had finally crossed over.

The summer following my wedding she began hormone replacement therapy. This improved her mood and her skin. If she was honest, she would say her life became easier once her nest was empty. She reverted back to the sweet woman I knew from my childhood. Post-menopause, she grew deeply engaged in her job, received a promotion and took her hobbies of sunbathing and basketball watching to new levels. She stopped cooking from scratch and began to serve my father meals made with boxed and frozen ingredients. A year later, she discontinued HRT when studies appeared that made her fearful of its effects. Meanwhile, my interest in my mother's emotional state waned and she and my father receded into the background of my self-centred twenty-something life. At some point, menopause was just a private fact of her new identity.

Now that I am perimenopausal, I too am sometimes anxious and can't sleep. Sometimes I feel manic. I have irrational bouts of quiet hysteria triggered by insignificant incidents like unfolded laundry and annoying calls from my ex-husband. I yell at my children. I have night sweats and hot flashes and my period comes and goes without any regard for the calendar, my sex life, or my schedule. Slowly, my body is transforming. Like my mother, I have a deep crease between my eyebrows. My eyelids look like fine crepe paper. There is a growing bulge beneath my belly button.

And I await my voluptuous curves.

Eddies

VIRGINIA BOUDREAU

It's a mackerel sky, mottled clarity.
Dark-fleshed clouds stewing.
The air is heavy with the cloying scent
of Gravensteins juiced to within
an inch of their lives on Grandma's back porch

It is hung with softness of doe skin jackets,
paint-splattered work boots in the corner.
Ragged geraniums in chipped clay pots
meld into glass, their yellowed leaves
straggle onto painted sills.

Through the window: those dark-fleshed clouds.
Their cores needling trees reflected in the mirrored twist
of a bottomless river. Like a menstrual tide it flows,
rich and pungent and teeming through troughs
gouged from hills of yearning, desire.

And, those dark fleshed clouds, always
in the background blooming on shadowed ground,
in eddies swirling toward wave after wave rising

from the deep end of the ocean.

My Mother's Skin

KATE AUSTIN

I'm wearing my
        mother's skin
and since I've passed my
best-before date,
her hands fit as if they were
        made
        for me

Personally crafted
by a tailor from
        Hong Kong
one who sends out
        full colour postcards
promising
the perfect fit

I remember
her hands, mine now
trembling as she
        smoked
        drank
her morning beer

from the sunshine
yellow of her plastic cup

I use it, she'd say
*because it doesn't break
          when I drop it.*

That yellow cup
Holds a faded paper crane
          a tarnished bracelet
          a bookmark
I lift it to my nostrils
and believe I still
smell her in it

I'm wearing my
          mother's nails
          her fingers
her rings almost fit
so I push them
onto my middle finger
too tight but safe
          the gold and
          treasured diamonds
shine
as she did

Her hands, now mine
tobacco stained and worn
with time and pain and
          for me at last
          with joy

I read between the lines
          of my hands
mining the veins
for answers

I map the marks
        on my hands
pale ones, dark ones
to find a path to
        my mother
        myself

Blue Thread

RONA ALTROWS

First letter to my mother

Mommy,

Why didn't you tell me about this stuff?

Wait, that's not how I wanted to say it. It's coming out all wrong. Too confrontational, too much shifting of blame.

Blame for what?

Time betrayed you. You were meant to become a grand old lady. Instead you were dead at fifty-nine. But you must have gone through menopause. How was it?

Nobody talked about it then. Tell me now. Please.

First conversation with my self

Mirror, mirror.

You can see the botched suicide attempt at age twenty, the seventy-two-hour sponge bath of your feverish baby daughter, the crying jag when your parents said, No, you can't go to Europe with a boy, he's sure to corrupt you.

Ahead, what? Decline? Illness? Dementia? Or greater control?

In childbirth classes the instructor says: "It's all about control. Keep your eyes glued on your focal point to keep control of the contraction. Control your breathing during the contraction. Rest between contractions to stay in control." The instructor visits you in the eighteenth hour of anaesthetic-free dry labour. You don't want to disappoint. You fake perfect concentration and perfect breathing for three contractions. "That's it, that's it, total control," the instructor says. When she leaves, you let loose.

Now, you hit fifty, career's okay, relationship's good, no more pregnancies in the cards, no more diapers, no more first-day-of-kindergarten jitters to help your kid through.

You have learned not to take crap.

Now what?

Your period doesn't come, doesn't come, doesn't come. You figure it's for sure now, you're done. You call your friends and say, "Guess what, I've arrived." Then, on Day Sixty-one, boom, you get your rag.

What kind of control is that?

Conversation with my new medicine woman

You're in choppy waters but you are a strong paddler. On the other side of this is calm.

You do have a medical degree?

Oh yes.

Why don't you sound like other doctors?

I breathe through my fingernails. I would like to move a small herd of elephants into my bathroom. I am the emotional matrix of my family.

No wonder we connect.

Pick a card. Any card.

First conversation with my thirteen-year-old daughter

"You still can't tell me to shut up, no matter how close you are to your period. You have problems with hormone levels? Me too."

Second letter to my mother

No wonder it's coming out all wrong. You never helped me get ready for this one.

Thanks to your two-year training program, I knew exactly what to do when the first period came. Look for the blue thread running down the centre of the pad. Keep the blue thread on the bottom, away from the body. Secure the ends of the pad to the clasps on the front and back of the belt. Make sure the long end of the pad is in the back.

We practiced a lot before I ever bled.

When I was four years old, you prepared me for motherhood with these words: When you hold your baby, hold her close.

But we never talked about menopause.

Can we talk now, Mommy? Can you give me the language, the tips, the tools?

First conversation with my friend

Eighty-five days. You?

Twenty-three. But then, the time before, I went more than three months. I'm all over the place. Plus forgetful. The night sweats are the worst.

For me, the worst thing is feeling misunderstood.

That too.

Are you taking anything?

Evening primrose oil, ginseng, black cohosh, devil's claw. All the beneficial herbs.

Dong Quai?

You bet.

My doctor says it's unproven.

What do Western doctors know?

This one is different. A medicine woman.

Consignment store incident

I'm standing in line with the skirt I have chosen folded over my arms. The two women in line ahead of me are about my age.

Looking straight at me, the salesperson says, "Oops, your dress is on inside out." I glance down, then head back to the changing room. The women in line do not giggle. For that I am grateful.

Second conversation with my friend

Morris has offered to take Viagra.

What?

Once a week is all he can muster. Always on Sunday night. An hour later I'm ready for the next round. I mean, one orgasm is not necessarily enough.

Definitely not.

Well, he can't do a thing after the one time. He's too tired.

And in the morning?

Still hasn't recovered.

Does he sigh?

Thank the Goddess no, he doesn't do that.

Rolly sighs. We get up in the morning. I'm fixing coffee. He'll come up behind me and pat me on the shoulder a few times, pat-pat-pat. Then he lets out a huge, heaving sigh.

Don't those guys know you don't have to be ninety until you're ninety?

Would it help to find a younger lover?

Out of the question. How could I spend the night with someone who's never heard of Otis Redding?

Second conversation with my thirteen-year-old daughter

I like it when we get along.

Me too.

My friends' moms aren't as open with them as you are with me.

I am going to share plenty with you about the journey I'm on now. Because when it's your turn, I'd like you to have some traveller's aids on hand.

What do you mean, traveller's aids?

Language. Tools. Tips.

Second conversation with my self

It's not my mother's silence on the subject, that's not what is making it come out all wrong. It's because I am trying to describe a work in progress.

Wouldn't it be wild to write about sex while having it? Then the sex and the writing would both come out wrong.

Still looking for the blue thread.

Thaw

ELAINE HAYES

Like a child at an arcade's claw game, I cupped my hands against the dining room window and stared out. It was a lunchtime routine I'd abandoned weeks earlier when we'd listed the house for sale, but on this February day, I lingered.

Slush now replaced the icy ruts that had forced drivers onto unintended paths. The warm Chinook winds, heralded by an arch that darkened the sky, had all but cleared the lawn of its mounds of snow. Our "For Sale" sign was down, I realized with a jolt. My eyes filled. Mark had changed his mind.

We'd told Scott and Jen — both young adults and away at university — we were selling the house because it was too big for two people to rattle around in. Mark and I agreed there'd be plenty of time, once the house sold, to tell our kids the truth.

"It's time to downsize," Mark told the realtor.

"There's too much work here," I added.

The real estate agent nodded and suggested a lower list price than Mark and I had anticipated. It made me wonder if we should have shopped around for realtors. We'd chosen our agent only because his personalized notepads regularly landed in our mailbox. We received so many, I'd taken the surplus to the fabric shop I owned and operated. At the shop, my employees reached for those notepads to record a phone message, or to sketch a design for a customer. At home, Mark and I had reached for them to scratch out our lists of assets and liabilities, inventories of who would keep what.

Without discussion, we'd signed the realtor's documents.

It was the first time the wounds from our callously thrown words wouldn't be mended by time, or by a soft smile or gesture, or by the salve of everyday routine. The *For Sale* sign, erected a few days later, gave our decision a sense of irrevocability. And, as I pulled in and out of the driveway each day, the sign reinforced my resolve. *This is what you want*, it said to me, and I found myself squaring my shoulders and nodding in its direction. *This is what you've wanted for a long time.*

I knew my sister Louise would blame my decision on menopause, but I also knew she wouldn't repeat my confidences. She was a lawyer and though her expertise lay in corporate law, she could at least offer some degree of legal advice. It was her other advice I didn't find so welcome.

Louise, who hadn't had a period in eight years, blamed her menopause for every twinge of pain, every occurrence of memory loss and every instance of poor judgement. Like an alcoholic who knows the precise details of her last drink, Louise could — and often did — cite the date and duration of her last menstruation. If pressed, she could probably remember the number of tampons she'd used that particular week of June 2009. I wondered if I should have paid more attention to my own last period, particularly since I was asked about it at every medical appointment. (Four years ago? Five?) Even my dental hygienist, before laying the lead apron across my torso, enquired about the state of my fertility. I envisioned someday I'd be bedridden in a nursing home with an aide spooning porridge into my mouth and the aide would ask me, *Dear, when was your last period?*

I had to start somewhere, though. I had to tell someone. And Mark and I weren't ready to tell the kids. Sometimes I told myself Scott and Jen would understand. Hadn't they witnessed enough arguments? Yet what if in the few short years they'd been away, they'd forgotten how miserable, how tension-filled our home had been? What if they continued to harbour romantic notions? What if they asked, *Don't you love each other?* My fear — of their questions, their judgements, their rejections — had paralyzed me in the past. It was the sole reason I'd backed down so often.

I announced to Louise I was dissatisfied with Mark. With a relationship that no longer exists, I quickly added.

"Menopause wreaks havoc with your head," Louise stated. "Dissatisfaction isn't a reason to throw away thirty years together. God, if every dissatisfied woman got divorced, who'd be left standing?"

Thirty-four years, I wanted to say, not thirty. And I wasn't throwing those years away. I was simply choosing not to add to them.

Louise ploughed through my thoughts. "Even after all this time — and keep in mind my last period was in June 2009 — my moods are still worse than during my pregnancies. Just last month I threw a battered cod at Roger. He was boasting, again, about our weed-free lawn. 'Look how much greener the grass is on our side of the fence,' he kept saying. Well, my biggest client had just pulled his account, the deep fryer was overheating the kitchen, and I couldn't stand to hear one more word from Roger about that fucking lawn." She paused for effect and I imagined her before a judge or a jury. "'Assault and Battering,' Roger said later, when we were able to laugh about it."

I stifled a smile; this was a look-at-the-mess-their-relationship-is-in type of story I once would have delighted in sharing with Mark. I shook my head as though water clogged my ears. Don't dwell on moments like this, I told myself. Besides, I knew if I did tell Mark, he'd make some snide comment about my sister's long-suffering menopause.

The next person I told was Rosemary, a friend I'd known since high school, a woman who proudly and often claimed she was happily married for twenty years. She'd grin, then add, "To three different men, but happy nonetheless."

Rosemary told me I should be grateful for good health and financial security. I should be grateful for two children who weren't drug addicts or dropouts or both. I should be grateful that Mark wasn't a gambler, a drunk, a cheat, or a hitter. And I should keep a journal detailing all this gratitude.

"I am grateful," I said. Grateful she hadn't called me a self-absorbed whiner. Which was, I realized, exactly how I sounded.

Unsolicited advice came from everywhere. My shop's assistant manager Suzanne glanced at my ringless finger and blamed fatigue. "Hot flashes can suck the life out of a woman," she said.

"But I don't have —"

"Maybe not yet, but just you wait!" She grinned, eager to welcome me into her sorority.

"You need a vacation," Louise suggested after the house had been on the market for two weeks. "Selling a house is stressful."

I nodded and sighed; it truly was stressful. Mark and I were treading lightly in the house. I got up early every day to vacuum, to wipe away dust and crumbs, all traces of our occupancy. (The master bedroom, though, was easy to maintain. I had moved into Scott's room and Mark had moved into Jen's. Our old bed, with its neat line of decorator pillows atop crisp linens, stood unspoiled like a shrine.)

We held an estate sale. From our newlywed days of shopping for our cramped basement apartment, we knew it would garner more attention and higher prices than a garage sale. We lay the knick-knacks and bric-a-brac of our marriage atop folding tables, donned gloves and huddled under the patio heaters we'd hauled from the backyard. We'd agreed about what to sell, what prices to command and what we simply wanted to be rid of. We also agreed to respond to our neighbours' inquiries by saying we were downsizing and moving to a condo. Those closest to us viewed the "Estate Sale" sign, as they had the "For Sale" sign, silently or with a few murmured questions. Others grilled us about the number of viewings we'd had or warned us about condo living and escalating association fees. A few wrung their hands and asked, "Who died?"

We emptied our giant chest freezer meal by meal, except for the seafood and the curry dishes whose odours would have lingered and might have turned off potential buyers. The freezer had come with the house and we had no idea if it could even make the turn on the basement stairs. We decided to leave it behind.

In answer to Louise's advice — yet more unwanted advice — I reminded my sister that Mark and I *had* taken a vacation. I pointed out that on every one of those fourteen days, I'd imagined myself alone or with Rosemary or with her.

"We can't relive our misspent youths," Louise replied with a smile.

I smiled back. This was an inside joke; both of us had married early in our twenties. Our youths had been spent pushing out babies or doing macramé or sifting cat poop from sandboxes.

Over drinks one evening, Rosemary advised me that she was doing just fine as a divorcée, but that it was difficult in a couples' world. She winked at the waiter, flirting, then whispered, "Just don't make any life-changing or rash decisions until The Change is over."

I realized how much I hated that expression: The Change.

"My doctor said a similar thing after I had surgery. But that was because I'd just had anaesthetic!" My voice rose in octave and volume. I instinctively massaged my wrist, even though surgery had alleviated the pain brought on by decades of quilting. "Jesus, Rosemary. You make it sound as though I'm incapable of thinking clearly because there's no blood flowing between my legs. This doesn't mean the blood has stopped flowing to my brain!"

At breakfast, Mark had wordlessly lifted his feet as I swept up granola crumbs from under the kitchen table. With the realtor's sign erected, I'd stopped nagging him to not overfill his bowl. I had given up the fight.

As honeymooners, Mark and I were that clichéd, old couple that bickered over every sink hair, every turn made without a directional signal. But we weren't *old* then; we were young. So very young. And in a blink, we were middle-aged and still bickering. Maybe I simply couldn't face old age knowing it would be more of the same. It wasn't just Mark. I was guilty too. If I had to pretend everything was fine, if I had to adopt a false behaviour every hour of every day, what did that say? We weren't husband and wife anymore; we were roommates trapped in a long-term lease.

Maybe we were never truly happy together. There was always an edge, and not the erotic tension kind from the Harlequins my sister and I once stole from the drugstore. Not the endearing dysfunction of those bloody sitcoms. Now that we'd put the house up for sale, though, we didn't argue. We didn't disagree about who would keep what. We were civil and amicable. There was no anguish. We had a simple, quiet routine. A routine of apathy. We weren't unravelling over this. We simply realized it was over.

I stepped back from the sink as Mark approached with his cereal bowl. He carefully washed and dried the bowl, his spoon and his coffee mug. He wiped down the counter and polished the tap and folded the tea towel. We were so comfortable now moving around each other. Why was it we'd never been able to achieve this ease, this peaceful, conflict-free existence? I mulled this over as I watched Mark leave the house.

As for menopause, I knew that it changed women physiologically and psychologically. But, maybe it was called The Change because women of menopausal age finally realized that change was exactly what they needed.

I'd told this to Louise on a day we were out shopping. I even explained how Mark and I had a routine of apathy. We were standing at the cosmetics counter sampling hand lotions.

My sister rummaged in her purse. "Maybe you should see someone. I can—"

"I'm not depressed, if that's what you're thinking."

"So you really think you'll live to a hundred and ten?"

"Huh?" I examined the freckles on my skin. How long had it been since Mark and I had held hands?

"You said you and Mark were middle-aged and still bickering."

With a finality that declared our conversation terminated, she popped a Xanax from her purse and paid for her purchase.

Now, as I wiped my handprints from the cold dining room glass, I thought of all the years I'd scrubbed nose smears from those mullions and those panes. When Jen and Scott were babies, Mark would come home for lunch every day. He'd always worked close by and I'd position the kids at the window to watch for his car.

It was a little competition, to see who could spot him first, and the kids were thrilled to spend time in a room normally out of bounds.

Soon after Scott was born, the dining room became my sewing room, a dangerous place for young children. In that room, I chose quilt patterns, measured and cut fabrics, and marvelled at the promises each bolt held: the ability to be incorporated into an award-winning art quilt or be simply utilitarian. A baby quilt that would be peed on, dragged under a stroller wheel, or wrapped unmercifully around a kitten's head. At first, I'd picked up the mess after sewing, but as the kids grew more responsible, I stopped tidying, even when hosting friends. "This is what I do," I told anyone whose eyebrows lifted at the sight of the sewing machine and the cutting boards and the numbered piles of fabric slices on the table. "This is my business," I explained as fabric fibres floated like dust motes in the sunlight.

Mark's habit of joining us for lunch at noon had long ago evolved into coming home to eat lunch with me on my days off. But now, with the house on the market, he stayed away. Our dining room hutch became once again a display case for crystal and china and wedding gifts we never used. I set the table for four. A family lives here, it suggested. I dusted the place settings daily.

A glint of silver jutted out from a snow bank as I stepped from the window. I returned to the glass and peered out. It was a corner of the realtor's sign, its post pointed skyward. Mark hadn't taken the sign down, I realized. It had fallen on its own. The warm Chinook winds must have thawed the ground enough to loosen the metal stake that had held the post upright.

I dialled the realtor's number. In anticipation of his calls, I was tethered to my cell phone; I carried it from room to room and slept with it next to my pillow. As I finished dialling, Mark pulled into the driveway. I drew back quickly, afraid he might have spotted me, embarassed he might think I was pining away for him.

The Chinook wind pushed and pulled at the air inside the house as Mark entered. He came up behind me and put his arms around my waist. He buried his face in the crook of my neck.

"You took the sign down," he said, his voice catching. "I knew—"

"You're home."

"Wright Realtors," a voice said. "How may I direct—?"

Mark took the phone from my hand, pressed End Call and then rested it atop one of the place settings. "I came back for my gym bag. What were we thinking, letting it go this far?" He shook his head. "I'll tell them we've changed our minds."

Threshold

JANE SILCOTT

My husband is a liar. When I complain about the wrinkles on my neck, he says, "What wrinkles?" Then I laugh because I don't want to press the point. Would it be a good idea to have him examine, truly, the decay that is my neck skin? Think wattle. Think chicken with pinfeathers that spring out overnight.

I care about these things now, but can imagine a future where I won't. When the dementia was first catching my mother, there were days when she might open a suitcase and put a hanger in it and then a shoe. A while later, when her mind clicked back again, she'd say, "It's terrible getting old. I don't know things anymore and I get so upset." It was awful seeing her in that phase. Later when she didn't know me but would smile when I visited her in the home, it seemed better. But maybe it was just better for me.

In childbirth, there's a phase called transition. The cervix isn't quite fully dilated so it's not safe to push yet. The experts talk about this as a time when a woman may feel as if the walls are closing in, and then they talk of the pushing that comes after as though it will be a relief and everyone in prenatal class nods and says, "Oh, good, pushing." And so begins another of those lies you buy into until you're in labour and realize that this "pushing" word is just another euphemism for agony.

Everyone yells encouragement at you when you're in childbirth as if you're in a race and so you do the best you can, but you want to scream at them all to shut up so you can concentrate. But you can't scream, because something in your personality or your upbringing has bred you to be silent when stressed. Besides, you know if you start, you might never stop. You might become the screaming woman, the woman who goes into labour and stays there.

Chaos, disorder, mind-ripping pain. That was pushing. And that might have been transition. I don't know if I recognized the borders of either during the labours of my children, but I recognize them now — a feeling that the edges are closing in. Maybe that's what my mother felt, and the hanger and the shoe in the suitcase and the following around of the cat with the tin of food were all part of her trying to make the walls bigger, trying to make sense of them. I'm not sure. How can I ever know unless I follow her into Alzheimer's myself, and then what good will that be? None, except to find (as I do, the older I get) how much there was to admire in her and how little I understood her when she was alive.

"We're giving birth to the next phase of our lives," a friend says over coffee — soy lattes, as it happens. The menopause experts would approve. We laugh and then she tells me she feels like a teenager again, and I say that makes sense. Though what do I know? I'm menopausal myself and sometimes can't remember where I am in a sentence. People say we forget things in midlife because we have too much information in our brains and some of it has to be offloaded. I think it may be because I haven't had eight consecutive hours of sleep since 1991. But the mind is plastic, experts say. Not the menopause or birthing experts, the brain experts — usually men. They note how other parts of the brain will step in and take over the job that an injured part can no longer accomplish. Maybe my mind is learning new skills too — like how to make do without the names for things, or my keys. Physically, menopause is the ending of a woman's periods, and scientists say the word actually only refers to the time when a woman's periods have been gone for a full year. Scientists call points like these "thresholds," which makes it sound simple (the same way that "transition" initially does). You imagine stepping over this threshold and moving from one state of biological being into another. And this sounds fine. Anyone can step. The body does it of its own accord, whether you want it to or not. Many of us step and then make a big hurrah out of it, as if we're celebrating. I even had a party, because it happened to coincide with my fiftieth birthday. At this party a friend gave me a book about women in their fifties who accomplish amazing things. Another friend gave me a papier mâché container shaped like an egg — and a significant look, which I ignored.

It's time to admit that the reason I started this essay is entirely superficial, which is embarrassing, but there we are. Some things, I hope, can be confessed and then dismissed. It began with a conversation with a man, an attractive man as it happens, but an academic conversation — the sort that can fire up in a hallway and spin out into the larger air so that everything seems to open up and new ideas rush in. We were talking about aging and then gender and so for me, the obvious topic of menopause came up. And because this was minds seeming to spark one against another in a higher, rarer air, I thought it was safe to mention something personal, so I said I was menopausal. It's not as if he jumped back or anything. He didn't run. But there was something. A squinching, if you can call it that. A momentary tightening in his pupil (only one, because you can't look at two at the same time, which seems wrong, but there it is — another limitation of the human body) and I felt suddenly and overwhelmingly ashamed. Why was that? Why be ashamed over a completely common experience? This man is a man's kind of man, all burly and hearty, but also sensitive and intelligent and so I admit I felt attracted. Or, more particularly, I felt a need to be attractive. But in that moment when his pupil squinched, I understood — perhaps for the first time — what the meaning of menopause really is.

In *The Change*, Germaine Greer describes menopause as "the beginning of the third age. The age when we are aware (finally) of our mortality, when time becomes precious and moves too quickly, when our looks change and we realize how much we'd relied on them most of our lives, when we lose power and identity (in Western cultures particularly), when we grieve for the loss of our fertility and maybe also for the loss of libido. Our bodies are changing out from under us. It is the change that ends changes. It is the beginning of the long gradual change from body into soul."

Safe at my desk, no mirror anywhere near, I imagine this graceful slide toward purity. I think of my father's skin as he aged, getting smoother and thinner, and the folds on his hands like fine silk, under them the ripple of vein, everything coloured: tea-brown age spots, aubergine veins like the rivers on maps. But my middle-aged hands are more like my mother's, my right index finger an exact replica, the slight bend to the left, as if it's not sure of the way forward, the folds around my knuckles, which aren't thickening yet, but tingle some days in anticipation of future immobility. The top of my back curves forward like hers did. My husband says it's because I look down all the time. He was following my mother and me in Toronto as we navigated a narrow, snowy sidewalk. "You and your mother, you never look up. What's with that?" I told him it was because we didn't want to slip, but I know it's also a dowager's hump and don't want to say those words to him: "dowager," "hump."

I know I'm failing on this passage, this journey toward soul. I'm stuck, not just groping for words, but stumbling around in endless circles of thought, and then into grief over looks, which is vain and silly and useless. I take some comfort in thinking that surely in this culture of plumpers and fillers and freezers, I'm not alone and that some part of me may be excused for clinging to old vanities and habits. But the phrase "aging gracefully" haunts me and I think I should hold myself to that higher ideal, forget my small vanities: my chicken neck, my disappearing eyebrows. Aim for a mindlift, instead of a facelift.

On the library shelves there are countless books on menopause, offering guidance and advice: cheering words about the benefits of giving up caffeine and red meat, taking up yoga and meditation. The women on the covers look competent and tidy, their hair neat, their faces remarkably unlined. Inside, they talk of menopause as if it's something we can manage like a stock portfolio or a new diet. If we eat enough yams, take enough vitamins, begin each day with sun salutations and affirmations. In theory, I'm all for health and responsible living, but in practice it turns out I'm the same person I was as a teenager: resentful, irresponsible, lazy, easily distracted.

In parts of South American and Africa, women are freed by menopause. In Botswana, for instance, the older !Kung women join the older !Kung men to tell stories and swear, to make lewd comments and smoke cigars. This sounds like a lot more fun than worrying about whether or not I look good or if I've achieved anything worthy in my life. In Western culture, one of the menopause books cheerfully tells me, middle-aged women free themselves from old patterns in their lives. They tell their husbands to do the dishes and they stop buying groceries and feeding the cat. They find new strength, shuck off old, inhibiting habits and become more fiercely alive and productive than ever. As I passively wipe the counters in our kitchen one more time because it's easier than haranguing the teenagers into doing it, I think, yet again, I'm doing something wrong. I can't even get menopause right. I think of my mother on the beach at our family's summer gathering place with her sisters and cousins, all of them in their upholstered bathing suits, the kind with skirts and lots of pleating. Their hair fluffed out from their heads in clouds of gray or blue, or plastered flat under a fishing hat with hooks stuck into it (my mother). They all had bags of knitting beside them and they seemed entirely content with themselves, their larger shapes, their wrinkled faces — all of it part of some big joke. Before dinner, they might have a large glass of gin and after, they might gather again for another. As I head off to exercise class, drinking a glass of soy milk before I go, I think of girdles, cigarettes, and gin. Why was I born into this relentlessly earnest time of herbal remedies and yoga classes? Why can't I take advantage of stimulants and supportive underwear?

My friends and I sit around my kitchen table lamenting our late starts in maternal life. The hard west light blasts in. None of us looks young in such light. We're wrinkling. The flesh is sinking. I have the beginning of jowls, one friend a series of crosshatched lines on her forehead. We talk about surgery, what it would do for us and then we change the topic. We're home with teens. Trapped, it seems, by over-sized toddlers who require our minds as punching bags, our spirits as invisible fences. Boundaries, the parenting books remind us. Limits. You're there to provide them. But what if I want to leap over those fences myself? What if I'd

rather be running or dancing or singing through fields of flowers?
(Oh stop, I tell myself. You'd strain a knee.)

On the internet, I find stories by men about their wives suddenly
leaving them at fifty, riding off into the sunset on motorcycles,
clinging to the leather jackets of unsuitable men, or wearing the
jackets themselves — and here I picture them gleefully waving
goodbye, leaving responsibilities and the dinner dishes behind
them.

On my bicycle one day a fellow cyclist gave me a hot-eyed
stare while we were both stopped at an intersection. True, I'd
been studying his calves, but innocently, I tell myself now — my
admiration purely aesthetic. I looked away, but, as I followed
him for the next few blocks, I imagined a life where I didn't make
dentist appointments and keep them, a life involving men who
rode boldly into intersections, light bounding off their calves.

Maybe the hormones are making small leaps, desperate last
gasps at lust and liveliness as I stare down the haunting visions
of old age: a friend's arthritic fingers in my mind's eye, another
friend's chronic fatigue, another's brushes with cancer, another's
missing lung, another gone, years gone. A tree she bought us as a
sapling full grown in the yard, a photo, her business card in my
drawer. Is this all we leave behind? No wonder we leap for men
at intersections, small dreams of our former selves.

I know I'm also mentioning this encounter because I want
to think there might still be something about me capable of
drawing a strange man. How strange? I imagine a Harpo Marx
type asking, but never mind. This isn't meant to be funny. It's
more pathetic really, a woman seeing the end of the road of her
desirability. I wonder if the bicycle man was issuing an invitation
at all. I could be deluded. My menopausal brain could be making
up stories to ease me through. In Susan Love's *Menopause and
Hormone Book*, she calls menopause "adolescence in reverse"
and says that estrogen is the "domesticating hormone" that turns
premenstrual girls — confident, lively, engaged — into weedy
romantic idiots. (The latter is my turn of phrase.) Menopause is
actually a recovery stage, says Love, a stage where we return to
our true selves. Who is that true self, I wonder, and does she do
the dishes and care for her family or does she go running off in

search of fields of flowers — or, in my case, mountain cabins and night skies filled with stars?

Most of the menopause books begin with an explanation of the female reproductive cycle; a few include a chart that shows four different coloured lines to represent the four female hormones: estrogen, progesterone, luteinizing hormone, and follicle stimulating hormone. During the reproductive years, the lines follow a predictable series of ups and downs. In perimenopause, the lines look like a two-year-old has gotten hold of the crayons — they shoot sideways across the page and then go straight up and cataclysmically down. At post-menopause everything goes flat. It looks like the heart monitor lines on a hospital shows when the music gets loud and the characters go silent. Maybe that's why few books publish them. They're too harsh, too close a reminder of death. They make me think of the vistas of grief that open at unexpected moments: seeing the shape of a man like my father on the street, for instance; or thinking of my teenaged children, their faces turned toward the world, away from me. To let go of people, first you have to let go of the part of yourself that needs them.

No one can tell me what happens to the individual cells when the hormones leave them. I'm not sure why I need to understand this, but it seems important to know what's happening deep inside my brain. What about those neurons that used to be flushed with estrogen at regular times every month? How do they cope? The medical people give me vague answers or strange looks. I search journals, the internet — nothing. Eventually I decide to think of my cells as little homes that have been visited by hormones for the past thirty-five years. Now the hormones don't come by anymore. They don't even call. I think of my cells drooping, looking for substitutes, sidling inappropriately up to other cells, or just lying in their little cell beds with the lights off and the blankets drawn up over their nuclei. I wonder how long this phase will last, this pause between infertility and acceptance. How long before I discover something to fill the gap, to spackle over the craters hormones have left behind, with knitting, say, or bird watching? I visited an elderly cousin last summer. She's sinking into Alzheimer's, but when she said something about youth and slenderness, her sigh was full of consciousness. We laughed a sort of hopeless laugh together, the kind that's full of grief. Maybe the years and years of hormones have left traces behind, like tattoos. Maybe sometimes they burn.

Some women say just before ovulation they feel a spike of desire and that even after menopause they have fluctuations in their hormones. Some time after the bike man incident, I sat on a small patio next to the pool where my daughter was having her swimming lessons. A young man entered. I recognized him from the day before, though it was a corner of the eye recognition and when I studied him more closely, I was a little surprised I hadn't taken greater notice of him earlier. He was deeply tanned and muscled, his skin glistened with droplets of water from the pool. He asked if the chair beside me was taken, then moved it into the sun nearby when I said no. I kept writing, ignoring him, almost. He sat facing the sun, his feet up on the rail, his head resting on one hand, as if he were napping. I didn't look at him, though I thought he wanted me to. At least that was what I imagined, remembering what I was like at that age, self-conscious in almost everything. A while later when he asked the time, I answered him and walked away thinking that if I were younger I might have woven a fantasy out of that moment, a life and a story. But I was more intrigued by my lack of interest and how much I was looking forward to taking my daughter and her friend out for ice cream. I wanted to hear their thoughts, glean whatever bits of their minds they'd allow me to see.

"Only when a woman ceases the fretful struggle to be beautiful," wrote Germaine Greer, "can she turn her gaze outward, find the beautiful and feed upon it. She can at last transcend the body that was what other people principally valued her for and be set free both from their expectations and her own capitulation to them."

Last summer I was sitting in a wicker chair on the screened-in porch of a rented cottage listening to the creek next to me and watching a wasp bump against the glass of the door. Cottonwood seeds drifted from the trees, looking like puffs of dust, sluts wool floating through the air. The day before, as the sun was setting and I watched through the small frame of the kitchen window, the light had caught them so they looked like snowflakes against the green lawn and the wood behind it, as if someone had made a snow globe and set it with grass and trees. So that next day I was still fascinated, still thinking of them as floating feathers or fairy dust, something incongruous and magical, something to be watched — carefully — and as I sat there I felt all the other moments when I'd felt the soft air of summer all around me and had time to look and listen, and so I was happy, really truly at peace with myself and everything around me, and I'd been writing about love and desire, which also made me happy, but the fluff caught my eye and that was more important.

Every day I unlearn. Today I read Germaine Greer again and am inspired. To let go of beauty is to find beauty. Yes. True beauty is outside us: we find it when we turn our minds away from ourselves. Yes. And isn't that a relief, to no longer consider oneself as if on a market shelf? To age gracefully is to say it doesn't matter if you become invisible in the world and it doesn't matter if no man except your husband (who is bound by habit and good manners) says you are beautiful. It doesn't matter. During childbirth, people cheer you on through the transition. No one cheers you on through menopause. You are meant to do it privately in the quiet of your room. I imagine the voices telling me to do so now (You can't write that! You can't say that!), but why be quiet about a birth? Besides, our bodies announce themselves. People used to call hot flashes "blooms." How apt. We flushing, heated women blooming out everywhere.

Perimenopausal I Buy a Navy Blue Blazer

SHAUN HUNTER

I don't belong in this expensive clothing boutique: it's for executives and society types, women who live more public, polished lives than I do. I'm underdressed in my loose cotton shirt and sloppy capris, but I ease open the glass door and allow the attentive European saleswoman to help me. This stop is a whim, a way to kill time while my husband tries on a new suit at the shop across the street.

I've bought new shoes, I babble to the saleswoman — a holiday splurge — and now, I want something to wear with them.

Some women, I've read, reprise their high-school hairstyle in midlife. For me, it's shoes — a pair of brogues, the same kind I sported in Grade 12, back when I was indomitable. Wearing them, I shore up my mushy perimenopausal self and sense the return of my adolescent self-confidence. But the shoes only get me part way there. Now, I need a blazer.

"Are you set on navy blue?"

Suddenly, I am not so sure.

The saleswoman looks a few years younger than my mother. Her accent is as soft and elegant as cashmere.

"Let me see what I can find." She heads toward a wall of jackets and I trail behind her like a puppy.

I keep my eyes trained on the racks of clothes and avoid the mirrors. I didn't come into this chic boutique to be reminded of my sagging, softening body.

So far, perimenopause hasn't meant hot flashes or insomnia, but it has ushered me into new emotional terrain. A story in the news about the suffering of a stranger can spark sudden tears and stir up the depths of my own losses. In the countless hours I spend as a writer mining my past, decades-old feelings come back, bitter and sweet. Sometimes the triggers are embarrassing. A line in a Taylor Swift song about her happy childhood sends me — every single time — into an aching about my own happy childhood. And then there are the sinkholes of self-doubt. Some days, I am almost ready to give up on this crazy-assed dream of being a writer — an aspiration I started to pursue perhaps too languidly and too late.

Thrown into this mix of emotions is a world that averts its gaze from aging women. I know the look because I, too, have averted my eyes from hormonal middle-aged women. Now I catch younger colleagues — female and male — scanning the room for someone more interesting when they are talking with me, or worse, staring straight through me as if I didn't exist. My body conspires with this slide toward invisibility. At times, the easiest thing to do is slip out of view in stretchy pants and shapeless old sweaters and let the boggy body-mind of perimenopause swallow me up whole.

The saleswoman holds up a blazer. "What about a nice charcoal? This season, we don't have much in navy blue."

My face crinkles *no*. I realize I am set on navy.

It's been thirty years since I owned a navy blue blazer, and back then, it was my mother's idea. I was a sophomore at a women's college in New England and my mother had flown in from Calgary to rescue me from a crisis of confidence.

"I can't do it," I had whispered on the phone.

It wasn't the work: a year into my studies, I was finding my footing. Now, I was struggling with my identity as a so-called foreign student. In my mother's hotel room, the story came out in jagged sobs. My closest friend, I sputtered, doesn't understand me. Nobody does. They think I'm the same as they are. But I'm different, I whimpered. I'm invisible.

My mother listened and consoled, but I wasn't sure she understood. In between tears and confidences, we went shopping.

I imagine how I must have looked to my mother that weekend. She knew I was resisting the prep-school style my classmates copied straight from *The Official Preppy Handbook*. My cropped hair mushroomed. My corduroy trousers were cut off and gathered at the knee. I had traded my high-school brogues for clunky wooden clogs and sported a cherished batiked silk scarf around my neck.

At the mall, my mother held up a navy blue blazer.

"You should have one of these."

My mother's *shoulds* were cemented in common sense, tested by experience and difficult to ignore. I took the blazer from her and agreed to try it on.

My mother's fashion advice was predictable. She had weaned me on black patent Mary-Janes and brass-buttoned wool coats. Later, as the fumes of the Sixties wafted into our Calgary suburb, she put an embargo on blue jeans and hippie hair. To her, the navy blue blazer she pressed into my hands at the mall said *classic* — a wardrobe essential for smart ambitious women. To my twenty-one-year-old self, the jacket smacked of giving in. I didn't want to lose myself in a sea of bent-on-success, conventional American women.

I remember my mother nudging me toward the department store fitting room. Inside the cubicle, I eyed the label: Evan-Picone, one of my mother's go-to brands. I fingered the jacket's plain, substantial wool fabric. Navy blue: my mother's colour. Sophisticated but not showy. Sharp and sensible. A shade that never goes out of style. Reluctantly, I pulled the blazer on and studied myself in the mirror. Whoever Evan-Picone was, he possessed magical powers. With one well-tailored garment, he had smoothed out the messy, ragged seams of my life. My blazered self was still me, but better. Pulled together. Self-possessed.

I stepped out of the fitting room, draping my scarf around my neck. As I walked toward my mother, I knew I would let her buy this expensive blazer for me even though I wasn't sure I could wear it. When she headed home that weekend, I stowed my brand-new blazer in the closet and tried to forget about it.

In the boutique, I peruse the sale rack. Shirts and jackets in turquoise, canary yellow, and orange — peacock colours

I favoured in my twenties and thirties, before I slipped into a decade of black when I wanted to blend into the background. I was still figuring out what I was going to do with my life after raising my children and I wanted as few people as possible to notice me while I did. Now in my fifties, I am experimenting with colour again — bold, beautiful scarves and vibrant, paisley tops — because, well, why not? But the blazer has to be navy.

The saleswoman walks toward me, her eyes gleaming with success.

"Why don't you try it on?"

Over the course of my undergraduate degree, I remember wearing my Evan-Picone blazer at least twice. Months after my mother's visit, at a Rotary dinner honouring international students, I spoke in full, insightful sentences about my expatriate experience. The next spring I was living in Toronto, finishing up the junior year "abroad" I'd cobbled together. After interviewing for a coveted summer job at an Ontario government ministry, I got the position. My qualifications were excellent, but my boss told me later it was the navy blue blazer that cinched the panel's decision. I knew she was only half-joking.

In the boutique fitting room, I slip on this new blazer. The jacket's pearl-grey satin lining glides over my arms and across my shoulder blades. In the mirror, I take myself in. My hair is cut as daringly short as I wore it in high school. I am heavier than I was then, but this jacket flatters my figure. The shoulder pads are slight, the lapels slender. The waist tapers at the sides, the back vent graces the natural curve of my body.

Much of what my mother and I talked about that weekend in New England has slipped away. But now I understand what she was trying to tell me when she pressed that blazer into my hands. "This bubble of emotion you're stuck in won't last forever," I can hear her say in her clear, sure voice. "All your talk about quitting … sometimes you just have to keep going. Engage with the world. Dress for the occasion."

I unlatch the cubicle door and walk into the fitting room foyer with its large three-way mirrors. The saleswoman waits to one side, beaming as if I were her daughter stepping across some new threshold. She scurries around me, smoothing the fabric, clucking compliments. The tailor is summoned from the menswear shop across the street and I stand still as she marks the length of my sleeves. In this magical moment, my mind, body, and blazer seem stitched together in exquisite alignment.

As the saleswoman rings up my purchase, I stroke the fine wool and imagine myself clad in blazer and brogues, claiming my place in the world. I glance at the credit card slip before signing. Perimenopausal, I will pay whatever it costs to make this navy blue blazer my own.

Bond

ELLEN KELLY

I am her; she is me.
Together we share a passion
for driving in the rain,
shopping for shoes,
and old TV movies.
I know her better than myself.
Inside me
her free spirit endures,
her strong will illuminates
unresolved regrets,
her determined pride
lies hidden in words I dare not speak.

She calls me friend
but I know her boundaries.
Her public world
dances to different music,
travels down a different road,
so familiar my heart breaks.
I want to run ahead
placing roadblocks —
signs that read

Detour,
Enter at Your Own Risk,
Beware.
No Admittance.
Stop!

But the road is dark,
the edges indistinct.
Her eyes are better than mine,
so I can only go
driving in the rain and
shop for shoes,
watch old TV movies and wait.

Reality Check

FRANCES HERN

Tom Jones
declares one of many posters
plastered on the washroom walls.

That white-haired old man?
Never!
I recall curly coal-black hair,
miner's shoulders,
tight trousers that set
fans screaming.

Up close,
from a better angle,
I realize with a jolt
how many years it's been since
I last saw him.

Salt

CATHY CULTICE LENTES

After my hysterectomy,
a friend dreams of us shopping,
filling pillowcase after pillowcase
with salt,
our carts so heavy,
we strain like shackled slaves
to inch them down the aisle.

She confesses, in her dream
she feared I coveted
her brimming cases;
strangely, in daylight,
I am embarrassed,
find myself explaining
I would never steal her salt.

What can this mean?
Reason says nothing—
her dream, her salt—
but a grain has lodged
in some dark chamber,
an irritation an oyster might
worry for self-preservation.

Does she think me greedy,
unrefined, untrustworthy,
needy on a basic level?
Why pillowcases?
Why so much, and only,
salt? We laugh it off,
but the taste lingers.

In the days of my recovery,
when medicines stir
within me a turbulent,
nauseating sea, I keep turning
back, a pillar of doubt,
recounting sins, those salted wounds,
no knife or drug can treat.

Child of Earth

CAROLYN POGUE

I have always felt connected to the earth. On the small Ontario farm where I grew up, there were myriad opportunities for absorbing that relationship. My earliest memory is of my mother kneeling at the rock garden, gesturing for me to bring my little tin watering can. "Listen!" she said leaning down even farther. "I think the flowers are still thirsty. Can you hear them asking for more?" I could. In memory, I still can. Menopause gave me a whole new take on that connection.

In my forties I chanced to read Ronald J. Glasser's book, *The Body is the Hero*. In it he wrote, "Not only does our blood go back to the ancient seas; we are also, literally, children of Earth. The carbon in our bones is the same carbon that forms the rocks of the oldest mountains. The molecules of sugar that flow through our bloodstream once flowed in the sap of now fossilized trees. The nitrogen that binds together our bones is the same that binds the nitrates to the soil." I loved that a doctor had set down in black and white that I was one with Earth. It was both humbling and freeing. I didn't have to "have dominion" over anything. Instead, I was one little part of everything.

The year I turned fifty, menopause began. In some respects it was secondary to my life at that time. Periodic international travel had been part of my history, but that year I took three international trips. To celebrate my fiftieth birthday, and my daughter Andrea's twenty-fifth, we travelled to England to see where my grandmother had last lived before immigrating to Canada in 1898. A few months later I went to India as a representative of The United Church of Canada on the first Women's Interfaith Journey. Because my husband was then national leader of that church, I later took the opportunity to travel with him to Harare, Zimbabwe to a meeting of The World Council of Churches. These three journeys were the opportunities of a lifetime. In between airports and hot flashes, night sweats and jet lag, I gained more knowledge about women, this good Earth, and my own body. I learned to ride the waves of menopause, to ski down its slopes, to enter into its saunas and freezers while still paying attention to the world around me.

The trip to England connected me to my maternal line of ancestors, the "flesh of my flesh." I told Andrea about the courageous ten-year-old child who became my grandmother and her great-grandmother. My grandmother had been one of 100,000 British Home Children sent to Canada to work as a servant. I had an inherent need to place my hands on the living soil from which she was born. I wanted to touch it, smell it, run my fingers through it, learn from it. And I had a need to share this with my own daughter, to reflect with her on our lives and what we had inherited from this strong woman. In my mind's eye, I still see us standing in the garden at the orphanage where my grandmother had lived, delicate blue forget-me-not flowers nodding in the breeze. These sweet little blossoms reminded me that my ancestors walk with us, into all unknown territories — of menopause, of loss, of delight.

In the autumn I left Canada again to go to India. The Henry Martyn Institute of Hyderabad had partnered with The United Church of Canada to attempt to answer the question: "When men engage in interfaith dialogue, they travel to a conference centre, make speeches, and hold discussions. Given the chance, how would women do it?" We participants did not know each other at first, but regardless of our differences, we immediately recognized that our experiences of the body and our approach to Spirit were very much the same.

To answer the question, one representative each from Hindu, Muslim, Christian, and local tribal traditions from across India and Canada travelled in India for nearly one month with a facilitator. (The following year we travelled again, this time in Canada.) In India, we visited rural and urban communities and met in story circles with schoolgirls, anti-poverty activists, and women working for literacy, cultural awareness, health, and peace to discuss our lives and build community. The powerful stories we heard were like water in a desert. One example lives with me still.

When one group of creative women learned that yet another local woman had reported spousal violence and had in turn been beaten by police, they made official-looking laminated identity cards for themselves and, fifty strong, stormed into the police station flashing their cards. They warned that if ever they heard of another incident they would return with 500 of their sisters. From this testimony, I saw how women working together could move mountains.

In Mumbai we met honoured storyteller and teacher Marguerite Theophile. Asked to define spirituality, she answered, "Like menstruation, child birth, sex, and eating, spirituality can be a mess. We need to recover our way of being at home with what is messy and reconnect with the joy of that." Here, I witnessed the rhythms of women uniting in our struggles against sexism, poverty, family violence, and underrepresentation in the halls of power. I thought about how, sweating wildly even in a cool, breezy garden, menopause was a big part of this mess. As with all things in life, a good sense of humour also helps. I was left with a powerful vision of the many different realities we live in and the many ways to approach the problems we face.

In December I flew to Harare, Zimbabwe with my husband. Coincidentally that year the World Council of Churches Assembly's theme was also the fiftieth year, known as Jubilee: "You shall hallow the fiftieth year, and proclaim liberty throughout the land." Personally, I was up for a Jubilee celebration! Fifty was turning out to be a remarkable year of change, learning, and celebration — night sweats notwithstanding.

Based on the Church Assembly theme, three hundred and forty-five Christian denominations worldwide were asking rich nations to forgive the crushing debts of the poorest countries.

Our Assembly also marked the end of The Decade of Churches in Solidarity with Women. And so thousands of us gathered to share stories, solidarity, and hope. One evening a South African woman entered the huge meeting tent tenderly carrying an urn. The water in it represented the sacred tears of women throughout time, she said. She poured out the water, proclaiming, "Enough tears shed!"

The vision had been named. I saw that my own Jubilee year was indeed a good time to begin again — both globally and personally. Menopause held the promise of a fresh start, and so forgiveness of others and myself made sense.

Part of the gift of those menopause journeys was the luxury of time to consider women's strengths and spirit during a period when I was emotionally wide open. I took time to reflect on how women are perceived in different societies and understand how the prevailing notion that old women are ugly, useless, and irrelevant is a bias of culture. In India, I was moved to see a young Hindu woman kneel and touch her mother-in-law's feet as a show of respect. Travelling in India and Canada with Myra Laramee, a Cree Elder from Winnipeg, Manitoba, affirmed for me the value of elder-led ritual and teachings. In Africa I met elder women from around the world. Another memorable grandmother was from Thailand. I was at the dinner table one evening as she questioned two young women from Jordan. "What is your passion?" she asked. "Where does your strength lie?" Gently, she guided the conversation so that they would gain courage in their work for gender equality. I see these women now as esteemed teachers.

My menopause years were full of the challenge and opportunity to deepen my connection with women and with Earth herself. As "weather events" took more precedence in the news, I realized that I was living my own personal Climate Change. Weren't there volcanoes, lava flows, temperature fluctuations, and floods also coursing through my body?

Duwamish Chief Seattle warned us long ago that what befalls the earth, befalls the children of earth. The kindness and nourishment that my body needed was actually not different from that needed by the earth.

My empathetic little three-year-old self, always resident in me, still hears the call of thirsting flowers. Even when we are living in life's rock garden, a sprinkling of tender care can grow great beauty. Childhood and menopause can help us remember.

Fact and Fiction

HEATHER DILLAWAY

List One: Things Menopausal Women Would Love to Hear That ARE True

•It's okay to be glad to be done with menstruation, the threat of pregnancy, and the burdens of contraception. It's also okay to use the menopausal transition to question whether you really wanted kids, whether you had the number of kids you wanted, and whether you've been satisfied with your reproductive life in general. It's normal to have all of these thoughts and feelings.

•You're entering the best, most free part of your life! But, it's okay if it doesn't feel like that yet.

•Menopause does not mean you are old. In fact, potentially you are only halfway through your life.

•You are not alone. Lots of people have the experiences you do. You are normal!

•I understand what you're going through. (Or, alternatively, I don't completely understand what you're going through but I'm willing to listen.)

•It's okay to be confused and frustrated at this time of life, or in any other time of life!

•You've had an entire lifetime of reproductive experiences and this is simply one more. How you feel about menopause is probably related to how you've felt about other reproductive experiences over time. It might be helpful to reflect back on all of the reproductive experiences you've had to sort out how you feel about menopause.

•Talk to other women you know. Talking about menopause helps everybody.

•Menopause and midlife can be as significant or insignificant as you'd like them to be. For some women these transitions mean very important things, but for others they mean little. Whatever it means to you is okay.

•Researchers are working hard to understand this reproductive transition more fully.

These represent the kind of supportive comments women might want to hear while going through menopause and, in particular, perimenopause. Items on this list also help us acknowledge that our bodies and bodily transitions cause us to reflect on our life stages, our identities, and our choices.

List Two: Things Menopausal Women Would Love to Hear But Might NOT Be True

•This is guaranteed to be your last menstrual period. You are done! (Or, a related one: You've already had the worst. It gets better from here on out!)

•Signs and symptoms of menopause will be predictable and will not interrupt your life.

•No one will think negatively of you or differently about you if you tell them you're menopausal.

•There are no major side effects to hormone therapies or any other medical treatments you might be considering.

•Doctors will be able to help you and will understand your signs and symptoms, if you need relief.

•Leaky bodies are no problem! No one will care if your body does what it wants, whenever it wants.

•Partners, children, coworkers, and others will completely understand what you're going through.

•Middle-aged women are respected in this society and it

is truly a benefit to be at this life stage.

•There is a clear beginning and a clear end to this transition.

•Clinical researchers are researching the parts of menopause that you care about.

This reflects many of our societal norms and biases about our bodies, aging, gender, fertility, and so on. This list also attests to the difficulties that menopausal women have in accessing quality health care or getting safe relief from symptoms when needed and notes the potential disconnects between research findings and women's true needs during this transition.

Last Blood

JOANN MCCAIG

The thing is, I didn't even know it was the last bleed. My body did though, made it splendid, celebratory, a Lucille Clifton poem: "Well so long, girl—" And it *was* beautiful: hot cramp twisting in my low back, a familiar muscular caress. Dark rich clots at first, a crimson so deep it looked black. And then a gush, a fiery orange gush, a rich bright swirl that mesmerized me as I stood, hand poised to flush. A bright fluid mandala that filled me with pride, made me think of Dabstract, those paint spatter canvases we used to make at the Stampede when I was kid. I wish I could have saved my last blood, carried it home in a cardboard frame, like a Dabstract. Displayed it on the dresser. I *made* this.

I loved it. I loved my last blood without knowing why.

Contributor Notes

Rona Altrows is the author of the short story collections *A Run On Hose* and *Key in Lock,* and the children's chapbook *The River Throws a Tantrum*. With Naomi K. Lewis, she co-edited *Shy: An Anthology. A Run On Hose* won the W.O. Mitchell Book Prize; *Shy* received an Independent Book Publisher (IPPY) Award. Spring 2018 will mark the release of Altrows's book of fictional letters, *At This Juncture*. Altrows is currently co-editing an anthology on "waiting" with Julie Sedivy.

Merle Amodeo was born in Toronto and now lives in the Beaches area of the city. She remembers writing creatively as soon as she could form letters into words. Her novel *Call Waiting* was published in 2009. The Ontario Poetry Society published two of her chapbooks, *Let Me In* and *Because of You*. In 2011, ten of her poems were published in English and Spanish.

Tori Amos is an American singer-songwriter, pianist, and composer. She is a classically-trained musician and possesses a mezzo-soprano vocal range. She has been nominated eight times for a Grammy Award. In 2014, at age fifty, Tori released her fourteenth album *Unrepentant Geraldines*.

Buck Angel is an American trans man, adult film producer, and motivational speaker. He is the founder of Buck Angel

Entertainment, a media production company. He received the 2007 AVN Award as Transsexual Performer of the Year and works as an advocate, educator, lecturer, and writer. Angel has served on the Board of Directors of the Woodhull Sexual Freedom Alliance since 2010. The foundation works to affirm sexual freedom as a fundamental human right through advocacy and education.

Kate Austin is a multi-published author and poet. She has published novels, poetry, short and flash fiction, and creative nonfiction. She teaches writing and is an avid reader as well as writer. You can find out more about her at kateaustin.ca or at her blog WritingandEating.com.

Glenda Barrett, a native of Hiawassee, Georgia, is an artist, poet, and writer. Her work is widely published, including in *Woman's World, Journal of Kentucky Studies, Chicken Soup for the Soul, Kaleidoscope,* and *Wild Goose Poetry Review,* among others. Her Appalachian artwork can be found online at Fine Art America.

Arlene S. Bice is the author of twelve nonfiction books. She also leads writing workshops and writers' groups; hosts book signings; and writes poetry, memoir, local history, and metaphysics. Arlene is a Board Member of the Warren Artists' Market in Warren County, NC.

Maroula Blades is an Afro-British poet/writer living in Berlin. Winner of The Caribbean Writer 2014 Flash Fiction Competition and the 2012 Erbacce Prize for her first poetry collection, *Blood Orange,* Maroula's works have been published in anthologies and magazines including *Volume, Abridged O-40, Kaleidoscope, Trespass, Words with Jam, Blackberry, Thrice,* and by The Latin Heritage Foundation and Peepal Tree. Her poetry/music has been presented on several stages in Germany. Maroula's debut EP-album, *Word Pulse,* was released by Havavision Records (UK).

Caroline Bock is the author of two critically acclaimed young adult novels: *Lie* (2011) and *Before My Eyes* (2014). Her short stories and poetry have been published or are forthcoming with

Akashic Press, Fiction Southeast, F(r)iction, Gargoyle, 100 Word Story, Ploughshares, Vestal Review, and *O-Dark Thirty*. Her poetry was nominated for a 2016 Pushcart Prize and she was the 2016 winner of *The Writer Magazine* short story competition. She lives in Maryland and is at work on a new novel.

Virginia Boudreau's poetry has appeared in a number of Canadian literary journals over the years. She lives in Yarmouth, a lovely seaside community on the south-western tip of Nova Scotia.

Susan Calder is a Calgary writer who grew up in Montreal. She has published two murder mystery novels, *Deadly Fall* and *Ten Days in Summer,* both set in Calgary and featuring insurance adjuster sleuth Paula Savard. Susan's short stories have won contests and appeared in anthologies and magazines. Her story "Adjusting the Ashes" was inspired by her ten-year career as an insurance claims examiner. When she's not writing, Susan is likely to be travelling or hiking. To learn more about Susan visit her website: www. susancalder.com.

Louise Carson's books include *A Clearing* and *Executor*, both published in 2015, as well as *Mermaid Road* (2013) and *Rope* (2011). She has recently been published in *Montreal Serai, JONAH, The Puritan, The Nashwaak Review*, and *The Literary Review of Canada*. One of her poems won a Manitoba Magazine Award and was selected for *The Best Canadian Poetry in English, 2013.* Louise lives in St-Lazare, Quebec.

Donna Caruso, an aging writer and filmmaker, rages against Mother Nature from her home in rural Saskatchewan. Her short stories have been read on CBC radio and published in several literary anthologies. Donna has won several awards for her work, including an award for Erotic Literature from *Prairie Fire.*

Jane Cawthorne's work has appeared in newspapers, magazines, literary journals, on CBC, and in academic journals. In 2011, she was a finalist for the Alberta Writers' Guild, Howard O'Hagan Short Fiction Award for her story "Weight." Her play, *The*

Abortion Monologues, has been produced many times in the United States and Canada. Jane has an MFA in Creative Writing from the Solstice Program at Pine Manor College in Boston and lives in Toronto.

Tanya Coovadia was a technical writer, blogger, angry-letter-writer-cum-fictionalist, and Canadian transplant to Florida who occasionally dabbled in poetry. During the writing of her poem "Always a Middle-Aged Woman," she realized her interminable hot flashes were not weather-related after all. A graduate with an MFA in Creative Writing from Pine Manor College in Boston, Tanya's first collection of short fiction, *Pelee Island Stories*, won her a 2016 IPPY (Independent Publishers) award.

Lisa Couturier's chapbook *Animals / Bodies* is the 2015 winner of the New England Poetry Club's Chapbook Award. She is a 2012 Pushcart Prize winner for her essay "Dark Horse" and a notable essayist in *Best American Essays 2004, 2006,* and *2011*. Her first book was *The Hopes of Snakes* and she currently is at work on a memoir about her horses.

Heather Dillaway is a Professor of Sociology at Wayne State University in Detroit, Michigan. Her research is focused on women's menopause and midlife, and she often writes about the everyday experiences of going through these transitions. She teaches about women's health, families, and gender and race inequalities.

Carolyn Gage is a playwright, performer, director, and activist. The author of nine books on lesbian theatre and seventy-five plays, musicals, and one-woman shows, she specializes in reclaiming the stories of famous lesbians that have been distorted or erased from history. In 2014, she was a featured playwright at UNESCO's World Theatre Day in Rome. She has won the national Lambda Literary Award in Drama, and her play *Ugly Ducklings* was nominated for the ATCA/Steinberg New Play Award. Her papers are archived at the Sophia Smith Collection at Smith College.

Elaine Hayes studied creative writing at the University of Calgary and the Humber School for Writers. Her essays and short stories have been published or are forthcoming in numerous magazines and anthologies, including *Grain, Somebody's Child: Stories about Adoption* and *At the Edge: A Collaborative Novel*. She lives in sunny White Rock, BC, with her husband Gary. Her website is www.elainehayes.com.

Frances Hern wrote poetry for both adults and children, and three titles for *Amazing Stories,* a series about Canadians and Canadian history. She also contributed two chapters to the recent anthology *Engraved: Canadian Stories of World War One.* Her latest novel, *The Tale of Irwyn Tremayne,* was published posthumously in 2016. For more information about Frances's work and life, go to www.franceshern.ca.

Shaun Hunter's essays have appeared in newspapers, literary magazines, and anthologies. In 2013, she was a finalist for Alberta's James H. Gray Award for her essay, "Skin Deep." Her blog series, *Writing the City: Calgary Through the Eyes of Writers*, offers a virtual walk through the city as writers have imagined it. Shaun lives, writes, and wears her navy blue blazer in Calgary, Alberta.

Sally Ito lives and writes in Winnipeg, Manitoba. She has published three books of poetry. Her most recent collection, *Alert to Glory*, came out in 2011.

Marianne Jones's poetry has appeared in *Room, Lutheran Woman Today, Wascana Review, Danforth Review, Zygote, Prairie Journal, Prairie Messenger*, and *Christian Courier,* and has won numerous awards. Three of her poems are permanently installed at Prince Arthur's Landing in Thunder Bay. Her collection of poems *Here, on the Ground* is available from Amazon. She is a member of the League of Canadian Poets.

Carol Kavanagh earned an M.Ed from the University of Saskatchewan, after which she worked for several years as a counsellor. Her literary work (short story, poetry, and nonfiction) has appeared in *Grain, Grail, Transition, The 13th Edition of the Canadian Writer's Guide, Chicken Soup for the Soul,* and *The Society.* Her volunteer work includes supporting her meditation group. She enjoys walking, bike riding, cross-country skiing, gardening, and having fun with family and friends. She lives in Saskatoon with her husband.

Ellen Kelly lives in Airdrie, Alberta and teaches creative writing with the philosophy that people create more effectively when they are having fun. Her inspiration comes from the wide Alberta landscape that she loves, and from the amazing people she meets along the way. She has been published and praised for her short stories, personal essays, and freelance articles.

Donna J. Gelagotis Lee's book *On the Altar of Greece,* winner of the Gival Press Poetry Award, received a 2007 Eric Hoffer Book Award: Notable for Art Category and was nominated for a number of awards. Her poetry has appeared in journals internationally. Her website is www.donnajgelagotislee.com.

Shelley A. Leedahl's books include *I Wasn't Always Like This* (essays); *Listen, Honey* (stories); *Wretched Beast* (poetry); and *The Bone Talker* (children's). Her work has appeared in *The Best Canadian Poetry in English, 2013* and *Slice Me Some Truth: An Anthology of Canadian Creative Nonfiction,* and numerous other anthologies. She lives in Ladysmith, BC.

Cathy Cultice Lentes is a poet, essayist, and children's writer. Her work appears in various literary journals, magazines, and anthologies, and she is the author of the poetry chapbook *Getting the Mail* (2016). Lentes is a 2013 graduate of the Solstice MFA Program at Pine Manor College and a 2014 recipient of a Work-in-Progress Grant from the Society of Children's Book Writers and Illustrators. (www.cathyculticelentes.com)

Margaret Macpherson is an award-winning author from the Northwest Territories. She has published four works of nonfiction, a short story collection, and two novels, including the De Beers Canada NorthWords prize winner, *Body Trade*. Margaret is currently working on her third novel, *Caribou Queen*. She is a storyteller, a visual artist, and a teacher.

Colette Maitland writes fiction, nonfiction, and poetry in Gananoque, Ontario. *Keeping the Peace*, a collection of short stories, was published in 2013. In 2014, she published her novel *Riel Street*. Her poems have appeared in *The New Quarterly*, *Write Magazine*, and *The Saving Bannister Anthology*. Visit her at colettemaitland.com.

B. A. Markus is a writer, teacher, and performer who lives in Montréal. In 2014, she won the Carte Blanche/Creative Nonfiction Collective prize and she was long-listed for the CBC Creative Nonfiction prize in 2013 and 2016. Her essays can be found in many anthologies, including: *In the Company of Animals*; *Salut King Kong*; and *Never Light a Fire in an Outhouse*. She has performed her one-woman plays across Canada.

Rhona McAdam is a writer, food activist, and holistic nutritionist. Her poetry has been published in Canada, the U.S., and England since the 1980s. In 2012, she published an urban agriculture manifesto, *Digging the City*. *Ex-ville* (2014) is her sixth full-length poetry collection. She lives in Victoria, BC.

JoAnn McCaig started writing before the first bleed, and has continued well after the last. In the intervening years have come two books, three kids, and most recently the founding of Shelf Life Books, an independent bookstore in Calgary. "Last Blood" is taken from her second novel, *An Honest Woman*.

Leanna McLennan's fiction and poetry feature visual artists, escape artists, and circus performers. Her current project, *Go See*, is a novel about the relationship between a white working-class teenage girl and a Métis teenage boy caught in the Reserve Scoop of the 1960s. *Seen & Overheard* contains observations made while riding the bus through Vancouver's downtown eastside.

Gemma Meharchand is a Toronto writer who was born in South Africa. She has travelled to many places around the world, including a return to the land of her birth. Her stories and poems are based on observations of the ways people are affected by geography. Her work is featured in *Canadian Voices, An Anthology of Prose and Poetry by Emerging Canadian Writers, Vol. One* (2009).

Noah Michelson is Editorial Director of Voices Department and Executive Editor of Queer Voices at *The Huffington Post*. He received his MFA in Poetry from New York University and his poems have been featured in *The New Republic, The Best American Erotic Poetry from 1800 to the Present,* and other publications. He co-hosts *The Huffington Post* Love+Sex Podcast, as well as weekly live streaming shows about queerness and culture on Facebook and YouNow. Michelson has also contributed to *Out* magazine *Details,* and *BlackBook,* and served as a commentator for the BBC, MSNBC, LOGO TV, *Entertainment Tonight, Current TV,* Fuse, and Sirius XM.

Lynda Monahan is the author of three poetry collections, *A Slow Dance in the Flames, What My Body Knows,* and *Verge.* She facilitates creative writing workshops and has been writer-in-residence at St. Peter's College, University of Saskatchewan; at Balfour Collegiate, Regina; and at the Victoria Hospital in Prince Albert, Saskatchewan. The editor of several collections including *Second Chances: Stories of Brain Injury Survivors; Skating in the Exit Light;* and *With Just One Reach of Hands,* an anthology by the Canadian Mental Health Association's Writing For Your Life group which she facilitates, Monahan has served on the council for the League of Canadian Poets, Sage Hill Writing Experience, and the Saskatchewan Writers' Guild.

E. D. Morin's fiction, poetry, interviews, book reviews, and essays have appeared in such publications as *Fiction Southeast, The Antigonish Review, Alberta Views, Wascana Review,* and *Alternatives Journal,* and her work has been produced for broadcast on CBC Radio. Winner of the 2007 Brenda Strathern Late Bloomers Writing Prize, E. D. co-directs the annual Calgary reading series Writing in the Works.

Lou Morin often draws on her Swiss army knife skill-set when it comes to books. A twenty-five-year veteran of the publishing world, Lou is currently working on a memoir and scientific exploration entitled *Stink: How I Came to Smell Crazy.* Her contribution to the anthology is an excerpt.

C E O'Rourke is a naturalist/poet who writes from a small island cabin, inspired by marine life, coastal storms, and the tenacity of trees.

Steve Passey is from Southern Alberta. His prose and poetry have appeared in over thirty publications in Canada, the UK, and the U.S. including *Existere Journal of Art & Literature, Minor Literature[s]*, and *Bird's Thumb.* He is a two-time Pushcart Prize Nominee for Fiction.

Carolyn Pogue is the author of fifteen books, a frequent writing workshop facilitator, and an advocate for children living in poverty. Her latest book is *Rock of Ages: The Oldest Rock on Earth, and Then Some.* Carolyn lives in Calgary, Canada near the Rocky Mountains. Visit her at www.carolynpogue.ca.

Roberta Rees's writing is described as musical and moving. Her publications include three award-winning books, *Long After Fathers, Beneath the Faceless Mountain*, and *Eyes Like Pigeons*, as well as many essays, poems, stories, and a thirty-minute film, *Ethyl Mermaid.* Her writing awards include the ReLit Award for Short Fiction, the Canadian Literary Award for Personal Essay, the Canadian Literary Award for Poetry, the Writers' Guild of Alberta Novel Award, and the League of Canadian Poets Gerald Lampert Award.

Lori D. Roadhouse is a Calgary writer, poet, aphorist, and singer. She founded the Hilltop Writers critiquing group and co-created the 2003 Writing Toward the Light Poetry Contest/Concert. She is a featured reader at poetry and spoken word events, and has been published in many anthologies, magazines, and newsletters and on websites, radio programs, and CDs. Lori currently has a manuscript under consideration.

Shirley A. Serviss is an Edmonton poet and nonfiction writer, writing instructor, and staff literary artist on the wards for the Friends of University Hospitals. She has published three poetry collections and co-edited two anthologies. Her work has also appeared in numerous journals, anthologies, and textbooks. Life, since age 45, has been a much happier time than any period in her adult life.

Donna Shvil is an artist and teacher, born in Montreal. She graduated from the BFA program at Concordia in 1986 and received her graphic design training at Dawson College, graduating in 1989. Predominantly known for her complex and contemplative figurative paintings, her work has been recognized for the portrait-like presentation and enhanced psychological realism of the painted figure.

Jane Silcott's book *Everything Rustles*, published in 2013, was a finalist for the bc Book Prize in nonfiction. Her work has won a CBC Literary Award and a *Room Magazine* Prize. "Threshold" was a finalist in both the National and Western Magazine Awards and won the Creative Nonfiction Collective's Readers' Choice Award. Jane lives in Vancouver and is a mentor in the University of King's College MFA Program.

Alison Stone is the author of five poetry collections including *Ordinary Magic* (2016), *Dangerous Enough* (2014), and *They Sing at Midnight*, which won the 2003 Many Mountains Moving Poetry Award. Her poems have appeared in *The Paris Review*, *Poetry*, *Ploughshares*, *Barrow Street*, *Poet Lore*, and a variety of other journals and anthologies. She was awarded *Poetry*'s Frederick Bock Prize and *New York Quarterly*'s Madeline Sadin award. She is a painter, a licensed psychotherapist, and the creator of The Stone Tarot. She is currently editing an anthology of poems on the Persephone/Demeter myth.

Rea Tarvydas lives and writes in Calgary, Alberta. Recent publications appear in *The New Quarterly*, *The Fiddlehead*, and *Grain*. In 2012, she received the Brenda Strathern Late Bloomers Writing Prize. Her book of short stories, *How to Pick Up a Maid in Statue Square*, was published in 2016.

Taryn Thomson lives and writes in Vancouver. Her story "The Game" was long-listed for the 2010 CBC Short Story prize and shortlisted for The Writers' Union of Canada's Short Prose Competition for Emerging Writers. Her work has appeared in *Room* and *Freefall*.

Lise Tremblay works as a wildlife management technician. She has a passion for art, especially literature, and has been writing the book of her life. Lise lives in St-Lazare, near Montreal, Quebec, with her husband Paul, son David, and their cat Léa.

Rachel Williams is an Associate Professor of Art Education at the University of Iowa and the author of *Teaching the Arts Behind Bars* (2003). For over a decade, she has worked as an art educator and researcher with incarcerated populations including juveniles around the U.S. She is interested in ethnography, visual culture, community-based art education, women's studies, and program evaluation.

Gerry Wolfram is a prairie poet who has lived in Saskatchewan, Manitoba, and in northern England. She is rooted in prairie landscapes, both urban and rural, and her poetry explores the landscape of human relationships, particularly the lives of women and girls. Recent poems have appeared in *CV2* and in *The Society*. Gerry works in education, advocacy, and community development.

Credits

Rona Altrows's "A sprinter with pluck and panache" received first prize in the limerick category in the 1995 Orillia International Poetry Competition, a contest that was run for some years in honour of Stephen Leacock. Rona Altrows's play/short story hybrid "Blue Thread" was first published in the fall 2001 issue of *Fireweed*. In 2010, "Blue Thread" appeared in her short story collection *Key in Lock*.

Susan Calder's "Adjusting the Ashes" won the *Alberta Views* 2003 Short Story Contest, and was published in *Alberta Views* magazine in November 2003.

Louise Carson's "Long Ago and Far Away" was published in her collection *Mermaid Road* in 2013 by Broken Rules Press, and is used with permission.

Donna Caruso's "Eating Beets During Menopause" appeared in *Carte Blanche,* fall 2014, and on their website at http://carte-blanche.org/articles/eating-beets-during-menopause-obsessions, and is used with permission.

Heather Dillaway's "Fact or Fiction" was excerpted from a longer piece titled "What Menopausal Women Want to Hear." The piece was originally published as a blog post at *re:Cycling*, for the Society for Menstrual Cycle Research, on November 7, 2013 (http://menstruationresearch.org/2013/11/07/what-menopausal-women-want-to-hear). The excerpt is used with permission.

Carolyn Gage's creative nonfiction piece was originally published as "Menopause and the Ugly Duckling Syndrome" in *Off the Rag: Lesbians Writing on Menopause,* edited by Lee Lynch and Akia Woods (New Victoria Press, 1996).

Margaret Macpherson's "Autumn Fields" was originally published in her collection *Perilous Departures* (Signature Editions, 2004), and is used with permission.

Noah Michelson's interview with Tori Amos, "Go. Rock." was excerpted from a longer interview originally published in *Huffington Post* as "Tori Amos On Taylor Swift, Fame, And Embracing Menopause," on May 5, 2014 and is used with permission.

Lynda Monahan's "Woman Burning" appears in her collection *Verge* (Guernica Editions, 2015).

Jane Silcott's "Threshold" was previously published in *Eighteen Bridges* on December 7, 2011 (http://eighteenbridges.com/story/threshold), and in her book *Everything Rustles* (Anvil Press, 2013). Reprinted with permission.

Photo credit: Calvin Thomas

Jane Cawthorne's work has appeared in newspapers, magazines, literary journals, on CBC, and in academic journals. In 2011, she was a finalist for the Alberta Writers' Guild, Howard O'Hagan Short Fiction Award for her story "Weight." Her play, *The Abortion Monologues*, has been produced many times in the United States and Canada. Jane has an MFA in Creative Writing from the Solstice Program at Pine Manor College in Boston and lives in Toronto.

E. D. Morin's fiction, poetry, interviews, book reviews, and essays have appeared in such publications as *Fiction Southeast*, *The Antigonish Review*, *Alberta Views*, *Wascana Review*, and *Alternatives Journal*, and her work has been produced for broadcast on CBC Radio. Winner of the 2007 Brenda Strathern Late Bloomers Writing Prize, Elaine co-directs the annual Calgary reading series Writing in the Works.